A SACRED TRILOGY

Monica Greaves

Published by

MELROSE
BOOKS

An Imprint of Melrose Press Limited
St Thomas Place, Ely
Cambridgeshire
CB7 4GG, UK
www.melrosebooks.co.uk

FIRST EDITION

Copyright © Monica Greaves 2015

The Author asserts her moral right to
be identified as the author of this work

Cover by Melrose Books

ISBN 978-1-910792-09-4

Printed and bound in Great Britain by:
CMP (UK) Ltd, G3 The Fulcrum, Vantage Way
Poole, Dorset, BH12 4NU

*This little work is dedicated to the World
through the Sacred Heart of Jesus.*

To Marilyn,

Thank you for your
friendship over all these
years.
    With love,
        Monica

30th November 2015

Contents

Acknowledgements

My grateful thanks go to my family and friends who have given me their encouragement and support so generously. Especially to my husband, Bernard, who has shown great patience throughout these past writing years. To Joan Burgess, my sister-in-law, I say a big thank you for pulling out the stops at short notice to produce a fine insert cover for *Christ Omega*.

For permissions granted, I would like to give my grateful thanks to:

Excerpt from THE HEART OF MATTER by Pierre Teilhard De Chardin. Copyright © 1976 by Editions due Seuil. English translation copyright © 1978 by William Collins Sons & Co. Ltd. and Houghton Mifflin Harcourt Publishing Company. Reprinted by permission of Houghton Mifflin Harcourt Publishing Company. All rights reserved.Paulist Press (*The Herald of Divine Love* Gertrude of Helfta)

True Life in God books (*True Life in God* Vassula Ryden)
O books (*I Am with You* Father John Woolley)
Ignatius Press (*Cosmic Liturgy* H.U. von Balthasar and Creation and Evolution S.O. Horn, S.D.S and S.Wiedenhof (Compilers))
Darton – Longman and Todd (*The Celtic Vision* Esther de Waal (Editor))
(T & T Clark) Wm Eerdams (*In the Beginning* J. Ratzinger)
ICS Publications (*The Story of a Soul* Saint Therese of Lisieux)

Armatabianca Organisation (*The Father Speaks to His Children*
  Mother Eugenia Elisabetta Ravasio)
Harper Collins (*All Things in Christ* R. Faricy, SJ and *Greek
  Myths and Christian Mystery* H. Rahner)
Oxford University Press (*The Cosmic Christ in Origen and
  Teilhard de Chardin* J.A.Lyons)

Le Milieu Divin Teilhard de Chardin
Every effort has been made to trace the copyright holder in
order to seek permission to print. The author would nevertheless be very happy to hear from any copyright holders they
were unable to contact with regard to this work.

Introduction to the Three Books

These three small works each express an aspect of God's involvement in our modern times in the lives of His creatures. God identifies with each period of our history as He walks by our side sharing in our struggles, providing solutions, giving us a way forward. The main themes are: the importance of recognising the human race's evolutionary development in our journey with God; the way in which God transforms His evolving Creation, through His Spirit, to become like Him; the acceptance of God's direct interventions in our lives as individuals and as a family of peoples on our journey.

The furthest corners of the world have been explored and now this one world is a multicultural place where people of every nationality live together. More and more, at least in general, we see ourselves as being responsible for one another at all points on the globe. It goes without saying that unless each person accepts that it is his or her duty to make the world a better place for all, taking it to its highest value as is possible in each generation, then we will struggle on with a murky, tentative vision of what life should be like, without making the real progress which is perfectly possible to make if we are clear-sighted about our journey.

The main inspiration throughout this work is the French Jesuit priest and scientist Tielhard de Chardin. He was born in the Auvergne, France towards the end of the nineteenth century and died on Easter Sunday in New York in the middle of the twentieth century. His spiritual writings were published only after his death but his scientific works, as a world leader in geology and palaeontology, were well known. Through his spiritual works he displays an invincible confidence in man and the world because he believed that God is a God of the future and God has every confidence in the completion of His Spiritual Adventure for His Creation. Consequently, Teilhard's words always lead us in the direction of God, as he saw himself as a pilgrim of the future. As a scientist he believed that there was no division between what his research had revealed and what God had planned for His cosmos. He was concerned with the problems of the world as any thinking person should be and proposed a fundamental solution to these problems, and that is, to allow the Spirit to take each and every one of us on our own spiritual journey through life, transforming us in such a way that each will play his or her full part in bringing about the perfection of the wonderful tapestry of Creation. He did not write in strict Gospel terms, but his work is illustrated throughout with Old and New Testament quotes, and what is more important than words, he lived the Gospel. From an early age his intention was to persuade that God's plan from the dawn of creation was to save, through transfiguration by the Spirit, the whole of material reality. This is not the way of traditional Christian thought, but he was a man ahead of his time and his thinking demonstrated Christ's words that after His Resurrection the Spirit of Truth would come and teach us everything. He took St Paul's two-thousand-year-old inspiration of the 'consummation of the cosmos in Christ', when the whole of Creation through travail would become 'All in All' in God, and applied it to the evolutionary journey of the universe (Rom. 8:20–23). There was never a gulf between his faith in the distant beginnings of the universe and his faith in its eventual 'extinction' revealing the Person of Christ of the Cosmos into Whom we are all transformed, fully alive and active in the Spirit. This is hope of solid substance for humanity and a vision with which I heartily identify.

For many years I have read the works of Teilhard de Chardin and wished that his vision could become the vision of our race as a whole. I have tried to present this vision in such a way that the science from which his understanding of the structure of life unfolds also reveals the spiritual structure of the human race's journey through time. This brings a sense of real direction and of inspiration for our world, because it is vitally necessary for a world moved on in its understanding of the evolutionary nature of universal matter to be aware of the spiritual dimension of our evolution. Our present understanding is woefully lacking, it stunts our growth and consequently leads us down unnecessary false trails veering this way and that, away from the true path which we are destined to follow – a path we must ultimately take because that is the way God has planned it. We can take that path which relies on our own tortuous decisions, bringing self-inflicted suffering, or, we can take the path which God wants us to take, that of partnership with Him in His great Enterprise, the Adventure of life.

With regard to our partnership with God, Teilhard's listeners would hear him say, 'We are not human beings having a spiritual experience. We are spiritual beings having a human experience', and that within every being and in every event there has ever been and will be, a gradual transformation from physical matter to spiritualised matter takes place. The ultimate destination of our journey is for us to be transformed into the Person of Christ Who is the Heart of the universe (Teilhard de Chardin, *The Heart of Matter*, pp.15, 16). This is not pantheism, which takes away our individuality and merges us into an indivisible whole. No, every being maintains its own characteristics, its own creatureliness but at the same time existing in the Oneness of the whole. Through God's Transforming Spirit there will be complete Union between God and His Creation. As St Paul says, universal matter will be transformed throughout time until God becomes 'All in All' through Christ (1 Cor. 15:28). This approach to the ultimate purpose and nature of Reality allows us to view God's activity and plan for His Creation from the historical, scientific and cosmic phenomena in an evolutionary universe.

The first section of the book 'Christ Omega, Belief in the Future' gives a brief overview of Teilhard's vision and his unswerving conviction that Christ is the Alpha and Omega of evolution – the beginning and the end of all that God has planned for His Creation. Christ is the way God chose to come to meet us. He is God, translated into human action. Through Christ the material universe is spiritualised through Love as it progresses down the vast millennia of time. All stages of the evolution of the universe, inanimate and animate, inexorably come under the personalising influence of the Spirit of Love. One Reality is being formed, and that is the Person of Christ. God in Christ Jesus has entered into the dimension of time which He made, and has allowed the human nature which He took to be formed in the dust of the earth in the same way as the creatures He made are fashioned and develop.

The development of human consciousness is the designed outcome of evolution in the human species and is inseparable from the spiritual. Humankind is the only creature to become capable, however, gropingly, to think of the existence of a transcendent Being. Human beings thus entered into a new realm of reality. Never could this be reversed, it might falter and struggle, and seemingly come to a standstill, but its essential direction is 'completion'. God's plan of uniting His Creation with Himself both as individual persons and with the whole human race will in the end come about, in spite of its apparent setbacks. Of course our co-operation in this work is central to its progress and final outcome.

The task given to the human race is to work hand in hand with God for the realisation of the New Heavens and the New Earth (Rev. 21:1). In terms of the dimension of eternity this has already been accomplished, God has 'made all things new' (Rev. 21:5, 6), but in terms of the dimension of time we have to co-operate with God in order to reap that reward. All our efforts down the ages have been used by God to recreate His Kingdom by spiritualising the kingdom of matter. Every genuine scientific research for the good of us all; the desire to build a more just society; acceptance of the inevitable sufferings of life – all of these are used to take us forward into the future. And there we can see, if we look, the unfolding of the Spirit of God, despite the darkness of the negative that twists itself around the Good. What to us seems like failure, God takes and uses to build a positive outcome.

The second work 'The Face of Everyman' is based on the idea of 'transforming union' introduced in the first book. It sets about describing how the Spirit present in Creation does His transforming work in us and in the material universe. The final result will be that Creation will reflect the total face of Christ, in the fullness of His splendour. The awareness of the 'within' of Creation, or the sense of the spiritual, is not something new; it is as old as the human species. It is only relatively recently, in terms of the history of our race, that we have lost the sense of the transcendent side of our human nature. Yet it is still very much part of us and an indispensable part if we are to live a truly fulfilled existence because the transcendent in us enables us to enter into the spiritual dimension of ultimate Reality, which is 'beyond' space and time and where we are destined to exist permanently after our biological life on earth ends.

Teilhard's understanding of the work of Transforming Union is beautifully expressed in his book *Hymn of the Universe*. I have used this and Scripture to best illustrate the transforming work of the Holy Spirit in our material world. St Paul's writings tell us most clearly the destination of the human race in the light of God's plan of Transforming Union which brings about a cosmic rebirth; in Christ's words in the Book of Revelation, 'a new heaven and a new earth'. This new heaven and new earth will be when God has made His home in every individual's soul, and He becomes 'our face', or rather we reflect His image. When this takes place for each of us, it is as Scripture says, 'for everything there is a season' (Qo. 3:1–8), and we each have our own season. There is nothing haphazard about our coming into being, just as there is nothing mechanical or predictable about each person's union with God. It is a very personal return journey, if you like, for each of us back to the Father's House. And we know that God has a specific task for every person for the good of the individual and for the good of the whole race and its completion.

The third part of this work is an attempt to awaken our race to the fact that God is present and working in us and through us for our salvation every minute of every day. More often than not we are unaware of His presence and His working in our lives but it is indeed happening. Christ makes it clear that He is our contemporary because, in His own words, He will be with us 'to the end of time' (Matt. 28:20). At other times He manifests Himself in dramatic fashion through apparitions and visions, through inner revelations and miraculous events. The experience of ordinary and not so ordinary people throughout history stands as testimony to the fact that God is not remote and uninvolved in our existence. Nor are these things unnatural or surreal, but are integral to what it means to be human. Our nature is biological and spiritual, and it is through the biological that we experience the spiritual dimension of our human nature. That is the reality of our existence.

God has always spoken through His prophets and His chosen souls to deliver to His people a word for each particular period of history. In this section I have looked at God's Works of Today, meaning by that, the kind of guidance and enlightenment God gives us, Who in His Absoluteness knows will address the needs of our day. The Word of God for our day has been presented here through the writings of two people whom God has given to us to support us in these difficult times: Teilhard de Chardin, a mystic and visionary, and Vassula Ryden, mystic and visionary, and also pre-eminently the apparitions of Mary the Mother of God. These give us the vision of what life should be like and what our way ahead should entail. Each in their own way touch, with the certainty of the Holy Spirit, on similar themes, themes which God wants our generation to become acquainted with for our spiritual progress, and the wellbeing and safety of humankind.

Teilhard de Chardin recognised the very real possibility of our losing our desire for eternal life, which would mean our disintegration as individuals and as a race. If this were to happen, our evolution as spiritual beings made in the image and likeness of God would be halted and we would become unthinking animals unable to distinguish between good and evil, and our end as a species would be inevitable annihilation.

Vassula Ryden is a prophet and mystic who receives messages from the Three Persons of the Blessed Trinity and Our Lady, precisely about what has just been said – that the earth is 'rusting away' for want of a proper relationship with

God to guide us through the restoration of the new heavens and the new earth. Vassula has travelled the world speaking about the urgent need to acknowledge our dependence on God. Happily, the messages of *True Life in God* follow the pattern of Scripture – they admonish and warn, but always end on an optimistic note; God is in charge and in the end He will prevail.

Evidence of our rejection of God and His indispensable help is all around us. There is no need to spell it out. Who would dare to say that there is not great unhappiness in the world because of our treatment of one another in all the various unjust and selfish ways? Yet, there is also mounting evidence of an undercurrent of a resurgence in our recognition that 'without God we can do nothing' (John 15:5) except create more and more unhappiness for ourselves as we become more and more disconnected from our true selves as individuals and as a universal community. Genuine hope can be seen for a purer existence, particularly in the yearnings of the young, to build one world for us all in union with God. The Godless pundits would say that religion and God are dead, but God has His allies in the young. At this point in time they are in the minority, who acknowledge God openly, but the young as a generation are searching for Truth, and they *will* find it.

Through very sound and balanced personalities Heaven is able to be present to us. There is nothing weird or cranky about their work. There is only the privilege of receiving God's Being through them. God has always guided us through His specially chosen people to teach us how we can be partners with Him in His work of salvation. He does not need our help, but just as any good parent desires that their children contribute to the welfare of the family, so too, God has planned it that His children should work with Him for the progress of His whole family and the cosmos, which is only the temporal home of every generation.

Together with many more in every era these are the people whom God has chosen to bring to us the fruits of 'the tree of life' (Ezek 47:12; Rev. 2:7, 22:2, 14), to bring light into our darkness, to give us the signs that the Spirit is alive and active (Heb. 4:12). We must rejoice and be glad for our God is not far away, but forever present with His merciful calls. Without His loving mercy our race would not have got past the first generation of human beings, but would have annihilated one another in our lust to control and dominate. This small work is an attempt to rekindle the flame of the Spirit by believing that God has never ceased to offer us an invitation to become partners with Him in the Great Adventure of His Creation and its final consummation in Christ.

CHRIST
ΩMEGA

BELIEF
IN THE
FUTURE

Christ Omega

The cover design for *Christ Omega* takes its inspiration from the goodness of life and mankind's journey, woven in many hues. The green background represents life: the threads interacting with each other in life's drama represent joy, peace, love, sorrow and faith, through time to its consummation. French knots have been chosen to represent humankind of different persuasions – sometimes moving in the same direction, at other times moving apart, but always vibrant.

Mary Joan Burgess

CHRIST OMEGA:
Belief in the Future

Introduction

Teilhard was convinced that St Paul's vision of the whole of creation being made new throughout time through the work of the Spirit was an evolutionary one, and was to be taken seriously and interpreted for our day so that our generation and generations to come could get involved in bringing about a world worth working for, where every person could feel his or her destiny was to be part of God's plan for making 'all things new'. St John the Evangelist too had the same vision as St Paul, a new heavens and a new earth 'where God lives among men' (Rev. 21:3), and it is found as early as Isaiah (65:17). And this insight has been an abiding one through the Christian centuries. In the thirteenth century St Gertrude was given that same mystical vision of the Divinisation of the universe as she saw herself 'grown up' into the measure of the age of the fullness of Christ. In our own day Vassula Ryden in the *True Life in God* messages was given a very clear vision of the new heavens and the new earth. Each individual who allows the Holy Spirit to transform them heart and mind into a temple of holiness will become a new heaven and a new earth and indeed a new 'universe', scattering the darkness and gloom, warming the world around them (Vassula Ryden, *True Life in God*, vol. v, p.101).

St Paul had not only a vision of the consummation, or the bringing to completion, of the universe in God but a very definite view that the human race is the key player in its consummation in and through Christ's Body, the Church, reuniting all of its parts, the whole creation, into an organism with Christ as Head of the Body (Eph. 1:9–10; JB, Eph. Ch. 1, n. 'k'). The power of Christ's Resurrection 'energises' not only the evolutionary direction of our own planet, but ascends, as it were, through every cosmic sphere, or galaxy, into the unknown and distant future until the whole of creation, animate and inanimate, acknowledges Christ as Lord. For every individual this would be through an assent of faith, and for non-rational creation by the Spirit shining through its material reality. God uses the natural world to make us aware of the Spirit present within every atom. Did not Jesus point out on His way to Jerusalem, when He was being criticised for the praise and adulation being given Him by the people, that if we will not praise Him the stones will, they will cry out in His honour (Luke 19:39, 40)?

St Gertrude, on the other hand, does not express the 'maturing' of the cosmos in biological terms, but only in spiritual terms, and then only applying this to the individual. However, by using St Paul's expression 'grown up into the measure of the age of the fullness of Christ' she indicates an understanding that finally, at some point in the future, God will be 'All in All' through the Redemptive work of Christ (1 Cor. 15:28).

So it is then that God's Enterprise is a two-way process. He creates and then invites us to be His companions in bringing creation to its final perfection. He clearly leaves Himself at the mercy of our consent. However, although He transcends time and space, as the Master Craftsman (Prov. 8:30), He works with us in the present, and influences that which still awaits us, no different, in a sense, from any other master builder who supervises the work in hand and yet plans for the completion of the building at some point in the future. The difference being, of course, that a human master builder can, from experience, knowledge and intuition, only predict outcomes, whereas God knows the outcomes and what is necessary to achieve His purpose (Isa. 40:26, 55:10, 11; John 1:3).

We must not, though, take the easy way out and confuse God's Being with His material creation. As Teilhard explains, our relationship with God is creature to Creator. He is the One who creates in the first place, animates and then sustains until His Great Adventure is fulfilled (Teilhard de Chardin, *Hymn of the Universe*, p.143). To read St Paul's words 'the whole creation is in one great act of giving birth' (Rom. 8:20–23) is for Teilhard an obligation on all to recognise evolution as a reality in our history and development, unfolding the ultimate reconciliation of all things in Christ, the sublime end of the Grand Enterprise.

Teilhard's personal belief in the future

Jesus said the 'Kingdom of God is within you' (Luke 17:21). Teilhard takes this to mean that the Kingdom is hidden within the heart of the world, and warns us that we must not obscure this reality by fearing to take this literally, and hence hold back from entering into the enterprise in which we are inextricably linked. It follows that, since our psychological make-up and our spiritual nature cannot be separated from our biological nature, each individual can be said, in his or her own particular way, to sum up the whole of created reality. However, we will only see this universal reality if we break away from our individual egoism and see the limitless spiritual energy which would be released by accepting that the cosmos is designed with an ultimate purpose in mind and that is the transformation of the universe to become Love in the Person of Christ. Evolution is God's holy work. He entered the world and became man, thereby allowing Himself to be part of the progress of the world just as we are. Jesus, the Word of God, is not only the end point of our Spiritual evolution, but of our natural evolution too (Phil. 2:6–7; Teilhard de Chardin, *Hymn of the Universe*, p.133). St Athanasius, 1700 years before Teilhard, expresses the same understanding thus: 'All creation partakes in the Word, and for this reason it abides in being.' And Origen, 1800 years before Teilhard, says, 'Christ, the First-born, is the archetypal universe, the exemplar of the forms from which God creates – He *is* the image of God, we are *in* the image of God'[1]. Teilhard further urges us not to waste the gift of becoming 'gods' by participation (Ps. 82:6; John 10:34) as all of us constitute the Body of Christ and share in His work of salvation for the world. He underlines this truth and shows us how wonderful it is that our existence is at once divine and material, transcendent and corporeal, bound up in terrestrial life destined for eternal life. He also reminds us that 'thinking' humankind is the 'last born' of creation, and the most complex of all creatures, and yet, we come from the same original 'stuff' of the universe. In a sense we are as old as the cosmos, but at the same time through the evolutionary process we are the prodigy of the Spirit. Consciousness has meant an uninterrupted development in humankind's creative (and sometimes not so creative) vision of building the future. In time we will become collectively aware that through our endeavours and struggles there is inevitably (although pains-takingly) developing through universal social organisation over the vast number of generations, a unity of purpose, a 'oneness' of being, a bond deeper and far greater than our own individual personality.

---

1 *The Cosmic Christ in Origen and Teilhard de Chardin* by JA Lyons (1982): 43 words (p. 126) By permission of Oxford University Press

Teilhard's understanding of the Church's place in Creation

The reason for the existence of the Christian Church, when considering the development of the human race and the cosmos as a whole, is the work of sanctifying creation to bring it to its ultimate fulfilment in Christ. Because the Church in the first place is the common origin and end of the human race, in so far as its creation was always in the mind of the eternal God as His instrument of salvation, it is the place where humanity must rediscover its ontological unity and salvation in Christ. We are within Him in His Majesty, and He, without losing His Transcendence, is within us (CCC nn. 842–5). Teilhard's thought was reflected upon by the Church at the Second Vatican Council and some of the fruits of this are to be seen in the Catechism of the Catholic Church. The Catechism makes some very pertinent points on the question of our place in the Great Scheme of things, it says, '"the glory of God is man fully alive" (St Irenaeus) ... The ultimate purpose of creation is that God who is the Creator of all things may at last become All in All, thus simultaneously assuring His own glory and our beatitude' (CCC n. 294; 1 Cor. 15:28). It goes on to state that creation is a 'gift addressed to man, an inheritance destined for and entrusted to him' (CCC n. 299), 'It has its own goodness and proper perfection, but it did not spring forth complete from the hands of the Creator. The universe was created in a state of journeying toward an ultimate perfection yet to be attained to which God has destined it' (CCC n. 302). 'God thus enables men to be intelligent and free causes in order to complete the work of creation' (CCC nn. 310, 311, 314).

Teilhard's inspired thoughts on the Eucharist and the Heart of Jesus

Through the phases of growth in our evolution and conse-quently the phases of growth in the Church, a single event has been developing – the full meaning of the Incarnation is being revealed – and it is this: Jesus, who after His Resurrection remained with us fully 'alive and active' through His Body and Blood in the Eucharist, invades every atom in each individual who receives Him. And moreover, we know that, yes, the bread and wine are consecrated in the Mass, specifically and directly becoming the Body and Blood of Christ, but also, through the influence of the Incarnation, at this same sacred moment in the Mass, in a very true sense, the whole of creation has been and is being consecrated throughout its duration, slowly forming Christ's Mystical Body (Teilhard de Chardin, *Le Milieu Divin*, pp.123–126).

For Teilhard there is an intimate connection between the Heart of Jesus and the Eucharist. Just as the Eucharist enters every atom in creation, transforming it, Jesus' Sacred Heart is the Personal Heart of the Cosmos, the centre of the universe – all is centred on Him, (Robert Faricy, *All Things in Christ*, p.17ff.). The Infinite Love within the Heart of Christ is the energy in which individuals and inanimate matter are fused together and yet remain what they are. In St Gertrude we also find this same intimate connection between the Eucharist and the Sacred Heart – the Eucharist is the extension of Christ's Body in the universe as the Bread from Heaven, just as the pulsations of the Sacred Heart of Jesus effect the salvation of humanity. In a real way, they govern the rhythm of the universe and its consummation (Gertrude of Helfta, *The Herald of Divine Love*, p.90, n. 16).

This is a vision of the Eucharist and the Sacred Heart of

Jesus whose impact should strike our minds with such force as to raise to a higher level, even to revolutionise, our philosophy of existence. Instead of holding a terrestrial worldview of history and human progress, this vision ought to be a wake-up call to recognise the inevitable direction in which the world is headed. History has its own *telos*, or goal, it is not just recording the past. History has its own journey towards fulfilment. God has promised us a new heavens and a new earth to work for. It is from the perspective of our ultimate future that we should be looking back at our present in order that the future breaks into the present, giving ourselves wholeheartedly to the creative activity of building the human community of Love and Justice with Christ, through Christ and in Christ. Even though Teilhard was an optimist by nature, he nevertheless was saddened that, given the invitation to participate in this Great Plan at the Heart of God, 'far too many Christians are insufficiently conscious of the Divine responsibilities of their lives, and live like other men, giving only half of themselves, never experiencing the spur of intoxication of advancing God's Kingdom in every domain of mankind'. Instead, 'we rarely find ourselves at the exact point where the whole sum of the forces of the universe meet together to work in us the effect which God desires' (Teilhard de Chardin, *Le Milieu Divin*, p.79). Given this unhappy fact, we must acknowledge that it is true that our knowledge of God is so imperfect that we fail to realise that in those areas in which God's will and our will are in harmony cosmic forces are brought into play within which there is no limit to what can be achieved, even given our human limitations (Fr John Woolley, *I Am with You*, p.116). Teilhard urged us not to hesitate to harness these forces for human progress and the progress of the cosmos, which needs us and which we need. Rather, at the expense of allowing these

to slip from our grasp we risk disintegrating beneath a morass
of materiality, losing sight of our heavenly inheritance.

The Incarnation – Christ is the Omega, or end point, of evolution

Teilhard sets out to give to us in our day an understanding of
the mystery of the relationship between God and the world;
this relationship exists and holds together in Jesus Christ.
When the spiritual/religious and historical conditions were
right, Jesus became Incarnate, entering fully into our human
condition. And yet, the vast expanse of the ages which went
before Christ's appearing was not without His influence or
presence. It was His future coming which manipulated the
biosphere to become such that instinct and thought were born.
Christ in His humanity followed the way of nature, growing
to maturity from birth to death on the Cross. His Resurrection
caused the vigorous stirring of the movement of the universe
in the direction of the Spirit. And since we, as His disciples,
possess the fruits of the Resurrection it is our task 'to make up
all that has still to be undergone by Christ for the sake of His
Body, the Church' until His Body, the whole of creation, is
completely Divinised (Col. 1:24), or, 'grown up until the age
of the measure of the fullness of Christ' (Eph. 4:13).

St Gertrude in one of her visions describes the Incarnation
and its effect for the Divinisation of the universe: 'And while I
held Him within my soul, suddenly I saw myself entirely transformed into the colour of the Heavenly Babe – if it is possible
to describe as colour that which cannot be compared with any
visible form. Then I received in my soul intelligence of those
ineffable words, 'God shall be All in All' (1 Cor. 15:28) …
As I am the figure of the substance of the Father (Heb. 1:3)
through My Divine Nature, in the same way, you shall be in the

figure of My substance through my human nature, receiving in your soul the brightness of My Divinity, as the air receives the sun's rays and, penetrated to the very marrow by this unifying light, you will become capable of an ever closer union with me' (Gertrude of Helfta, *The Herald of Divine Love*, p.104).

God becoming man, identifying Himself entirely with humanity in history, shows that this 'was no random event, but an intervention of deepest and universal significance. Love, tenderly and patiently watching over the human race during its development was compelled to submit to earth's experience' (Fr John Woolley, *I Am With You*, p.192). St Athanasius puts it succinctly, 'God becomes man so that man might become God'. Christ's presence was not and is not simply passive, but 'alive and active', animating the whole universe, driving it forward to return it to God, bringing it to perfection through the aeons of time (Col. 1:17–20; John 1:4, 9, 12, 16).

Love at the heart of the universe is the energy which draws creation to its evolutionary final end. Love and thought cannot be separated from spirit. The Christian community is commanded by Christ to live by love with Him as the Church's Guide, leading us on to full union with the Blessed Trinity. Love penetrating matter inexorably unfolds in higher and deeper levels of spirit. Creation's progress to unity with God comes stealthily in every atom and molecule which are being transformed and spiritual-ised. Christ's abiding presence through the Incarnation is the bedrock from which we work to perfect His creation. Having faith that He is active in our cause should spur us on to attempt-ing great things for Him. The new heavens and the new earth that He promised us is within our grasp – He has confidence in us to do this, but only if we abide in Him and He in us (John 15:1–10). The earth can only become new by allowing Heaven into our hearts. This responsibility is ours and ours alone.

God's Plan for Humankind through the process of Life Development

The biological development of the world was designed solely for the eventual appearance of humankind. Biological progress thus far can be verified by science, but the creation of each person, that is, the soul of the human person, cannot – this is the work of the Spirit, which is beyond the scope of science (Gen. 1:26–31; Teilhard de Chardin, *Hymn of the Universe*, p.100). 'The clay became man at that moment in which a being for the first time was capable of forming, however dimly, the thought of 'God'. The first 'Thou' that – however stammeringly – was said by human lips to God marks the moment in which spirit arose in the world' (S.O. Horn and S. Wiedenhofer, *Creation and Evolution*, p.15). Humankind is the only creature who was destined to form a personal relationship with God, because in man there is the fullest development of consciousness. Every other creature from fishes to mammals and even the most sophisticated primates have all halted in their development at some point along that line of evolution. Humankind alone has succeeded in crossing the threshold of consciousness, enabling it to rationalise to the extent to which it does. We are able to live a life of self-development through abstract thought, logic, reason, choice and invention, science, art, and most crucial of all, *love*, with all its complexities. Having the capacity to love takes us into the realm of an inner life. That inner life is the source of our self-awareness and the knowledge that we possess the ability to transcend our earthly life through prayer and meditation. In other words, we are able to enter into that dimension of existence which we call eternity, and in that dimension to develop our relationship with God, Who above all else is 'Person' in the absolute sense of the word. To say that this is not a phenomenon of life belonging to humankind alone is to turn our face away from the truth and to bury our heads in the sand. Hans Urs von Balthasar explains this same idea found in Teilhard's writings in the thought of Maximum the Confessor: because we live in a transcendent cosmic context our species alone can conceive of an ultimate reality which includes other dimensions of existence, thereby, it is fundamental to our nature, and not in the nature of other creatures, to be in contact with the whole of reality (Hans Urs von Balthasar, *Cosmic Liturgy*, p.287).

Pope Benedict in his address to the Pontifical Academy of Sciences points out that together science and philosophy/theology can help us understand that there is a difference between evolution simply as a succession in space and time and evolution as a purposeful act of creation which from the very beginning involves created beings in the existence of eternal God (Pope Benedict, *Address*, 6th Nov. 2006). St Paul himself says, 'It is not the spiritual which is first but the physical, and *then* the spiritual' (1 Cor. 15:46). If we see things the other way around, we cannot hold to God having created the natural world first, and then, gives creation the Spirit of grace through Whom we are able to share God's life (Joseph Ratzinger, *In the Beginning*, p.94). It is not a chance happening that only the human community reflects globally upon itself and that only the human community has developed as a social group globally. Therefore, since life has not just evolved without purpose, but has a definite reference point, we must do everything in our power as individuals to take the human community forward to its goal. It is only within the solidarity of our race as a whole that the individual can become fully the person he or she was intended to become. We achieve this by recognising that we are a race destined through time to, literally, bring one another to heaven with us as the Body of Christ and this cannot be done if we do not succeed in trying our level best to reach 'perfect' social cohesion wherein every person has at least the knowledge and opportunity to have heaven as his or her desired end (Teilhard de Chardin, *The Future of Man*, pp.223–7).

The Church

Teilhard's relationship with the Catholic Church was one of tension, love and frustration. He believed that the Church is the axis of Christianity, but because it is incarnate in the world, it grows and develops, it is not static, but is subject to historical conditions, but nevertheless, is where Christianity is found in its fullness.

This being the case, the Church is to be, as it were, the soul of human society in its renewal by Christ and transformation into the family of God (CCC n. 854). The Church also is not a chance happening nor an anomaly in the development of human socialisation, but the 'place' where Divine grace and human reflection gradually achieve human unity. It is the engine which drives our race, however falteringly, towards its eternal destiny.

There is, though, among the huge variety of believers within the Church, a crisis of faith and belief in our future through the process of evolution. For the most part, the ordinary Christian has not recognised the immensity of God's plan from the beginning, and therefore is not spurred on to play a full part in completing the Adventure of the human race hand in hand with Christ, really and truly building the Cosmic Body of Christ – a universal project in which each of us has a unique part to play (Teilhard de Chardin, *The Future of Man*, p.266ff.). On the one hand the Church unfailingly teaches that our future as human persons lies beyond our physical death in the realm of eternity. But, as yet, it does not acknowledge that this is achieved through a synthesis of biological/psychic development and the workings of grace together. Rather, it rightly teaches the priority of grace, but through an already complete psychic centre, and not as part and parcel of a continuous growth of consciousness in the individual and in humanity as a whole. The consummation of the Kingdom according to Teilhard will come about when humankind has biologically reached its point of full growth in its mental capacity through Christ's saving work in the world. Christ is the architect of creation, the energy through which evolution takes its course over the ages, and the Redeemer through Whom the whole of creation is returned to the Father in its perfection. How disappointed we will be when we get to Heaven and see, if we had only realised, what a wonderful opportunity had been offered to us to take part in, not only such a noble work, but the very work God intended each of us to do from the moment of our creation, and that was to be co-creators, co-redeemers and co-consummators with Him (Phil. 2:13–16; Eph. 1:23, 4:13–16; 1 Cor. 15:22–8).

God's influence in the world is unfailing because He transcends time. He can shape the present and prepare the future through His own infinite, perfect Love and our own finite, imperfect love co-operating with Him. The Church, being God's instrument for His action (though not the only one) at the heart of the natural and supernatural universe is the vehicle of transformation through prayer and work (CCC n. 760). Prayer is our small effort at co-operation, it is the tool which God uses to rearrange events, drawing good out of chaos to take creation forward. The Church's liturgy, and par excellence the Mass, effects the divinisation of existence because it absorbs the entire creation into the mystery of the two natures of Christ, His human nature and His divine nature. The Church in all its variety, and in spite of failures, is already the image and likeness of God, He holds it together and brings it into the oneness of unity, but 'still leaves to each being its own being and its own place' (CCC nn. 1080–86; Hans Urs von Balthasar, *Cosmic Liturgy*, p.322).

The Christianity of Tomorrow

Other religions cannot account for the evolutionary development of the human race along the lines of the rise of the Spirit. That is because they hold to a completed, static universe. Teilhard confidently asserts that Christianity is the only religion that can explain a universe in movement towards a predestined consummation because its doctrine is in the main stream of evolution, that is, Creation, Incarnation and Redemption.

The Christianity of tomorrow will teach the Good News that the natural effort of life is in itself vital if universal development is to reach its intended Term in Christ since He is that Term. It is our privilege to work for the completion of Christ's Body, and by completion is meant that each person's desire for self-fulfilment can only be realised by accepting that we are rooted in and evolve with the natural universe. Through matter (Christ's human nature) and through Spirit (Christ's Divine nature) we work towards the creation of a supreme Summit of consciousness. Christianity needs to show itself as it truly is, the Religion of tomorrow. The Religion which teaches the immense enterprise we are involved in, the ultimate perfecting of the human person seen in our journey with the world in movement. The consequences for humanity perfecting itself through the energy of Christ's Cross and Resurrection, never to be checked in its outpouring, will be self-sacrificial Love expressed in universal concern for true justice for everyone, which will inevitably result in living in harmony with the natural world (Teilhard de Chardin, *The Heart of Matter*, p.222).

Marxism, Humanism, Atheism, 'religions' only of matter, dehumanise us with their stunted view of the human person. They cannot inspire humanity to rise to the challenge of perfecting the world though their full human nature of matter and spirit. Instead, they urge us to look no further than the earth's horizon because this is the extent of our existence; this is the extent to which we are able to love, or be self-fulfilled. Death means death and not eternal life wherein we are immersed in Universal Love entirely committed to the wellbeing of those still on their earthly journey.

On the other hand, other religions, Christianity included, tend to blur our vision of the depth of reality through narrowing the horizon by focusing largely on our immortality and our eternal end. It is as if we were 'unrelated' to our earthly home, somehow in a foreign land through which we must journey before we reach our goal. This shows a lack of appreciation of the natural cycle in which we are irrevocably bound to the very matter through which we grow and live, yield our vitality to old age, die to our attachment to this world and rise again perfected in spirit to live a life of untainted Love in our Heavenly home (Teilhard de Chardin, *The Heart of Matter*, p.98).

Traditional theology ties us almost exclusively to our glory in Heaven, this earth being essentially of little use to us spiritually. To situate our history outside an evolutionary perspective makes a correct reading of our race as a developing global community of families theologically difficult. To speak of the 'family of man', without acknowledging our common biological family tie from our earliest embryonic stage in primitive matter to reaching maturity in the far distant future, misses the important fact that we have always been a family community with a common end. This traditional view does not express the meaning of the present and the life of the world to come in language which explains our 'family's' history in terms of an emerging unification over an immense stretch of time through the God-designed process of socialisation, rather, it focuses on our future as individuals and 'other worldly'. We are saved as individuals, yes, but always within, and not separate from, the whole Family. Since the 1960s and the Second Vatican Council there has been a shift in the Church's presentation of the goal of our history, the future focal point of the whole human community, particularly in the Church's pastoral document *Gaudium et spes, Pastoral Constitution of the Church in the Modern World.* The document describes the profound changes experienced by society at large and the difficulties that result from these changes as 'the human race passes through a new stage in its history' (Section 4). Civilisation, and indeed, the universe itself is seen as converging in an historical evolutionary process towards its ultimate goal, Jesus Christ risen, and the final reconciliation of all things in Him.

It is obvious that over the vast expanse of time the process of evolution has produced waste and failure. In non-living things, this waste takes the form of decomposition. In human beings it takes the form of unproductive struggle, self-inflicted suffering and death. And in the moral order, in the realm of human freedom, it takes the form of sin. Failure to act for the good of the whole family is an abuse of our freedom which turns us away from God and results in disunion and disorder. Teilhard saw this as an inevitable outcome of the human race progressing towards ever higher and higher unity. He believed that evil in the world is the absence of union causing disharmony and stunted growth. Sin is the precise opposite of the driving force towards union, which is love. Love is the antidote to disunion, because love unites and automatically chooses union. Sin separates and chooses disintegration and disorder (Robert Faricy, *All Things in Christ*, p.52ff.).

The Heart of Jesus

If Teilhard saw love as the source of the driving force towards union, He also saw that that love is no less than a 'supra-personal' heart of matter, the Heart of Jesus, the God Man, wherein every beat since the beginning of time shapes and transforms the universe. This is a vision for our time, a reality for a world confused about the meaning of its existence to contemplate. It is a personalised universe because it radiates the Love of God through the Heart of Christ: a finite world, yes, that can be explained in terms of physics and chemistry by finite minds, but which cannot explain or understand fully the Infinite Mind of God who holds the world in existence. It is only faith in God and His Love which impels us to go beyond that which we can understand through science and strike out towards the uncharted domain of Love, wherein we will find life's real meaning and purpose.

St Gertrude too, 700 years earlier, was given a prophetic vision for our time, through St John the Evangelist, of the things God had 'hidden' in His Sacred Heart. St John, when asked by St Gertrude why the Evangelist had not spoken of these things before, explained: 'My mission was to deliver to the Church, in her first age, a simple word on the uncreated Word of God the Father that would afford the whole of humanity enough to contemplate until the end of the world, yet without any person ever fully grasping it. But to tell of the pulsations of the Heart of Jesus has been reserved for modern times so that in hearing these things, the world already old and growing cold in the love of God, may be rekindled and grow warm again' (Vassula Ryden, *True Life in God*, vol. v, p.85).

Teilhard's vision brings hope for our world today and for future generations through this fresh understanding of God's evolving creation and the Love at the very heart of it, by which

our very existence is upheld. In his book *The Heart of Matter*
Teilhard explains that for him the Sacred Heart of Jesus was
the source of Energy through which the Fire of His Love
penetrates and changes into love everything within the cosmos
from its primeval beginnings to its appointed end. As he sat
in prayer in front of a picture of Jesus revealing His heart of
fire, he describes how this familiar image suddenly became
radiant, transmitting rays of light. The heart itself no longer
retained its outward form but became an intense furnace of
fire whose magnificence enveloped the whole painting, first the
portrait then the background and beyond out into the universe.
Everything that lay within its path was being transformed into
His Likeness, even inanimate matter was showing forth the
Glory of God. Jesus Himself was immersing Himself in every
created thing until He likened us as we likened Him, extending
to the remotest ages still to come ('I have come to bring fire
to the earth, and how I wish it were blazing already!', Luke
12:49). In the vast arrangement of the cosmos constructive and
destructive events alike are penetrated by this unifying force,
until that age when the cosmos is fully and finally personalised (Teilhard de Chardin, *The Heart of Matter*, p.44ff.). The
Incarnation of God in Jesus has effected the realisation of this
complex whole. It is in the Heart of Jesus, Divine and human,
Heaven touching the earth, wherein the synthesis between
the personal and matter takes place to become Love (Robert
Faricy, *All Things in Christ*, p.17).

This must be seen in the context of the final destiny both of
the individual soul and the family of humankind in general and
the end and fate of the physical world. In Teilhard's spiritual life,
even from a young boy, the traditional God of the Transcendent
and the God of the aeons ahead was always the same God
working in his life. He could not worship anything less than

the One God of Heaven and the One God who transforms what awaits us and the whole of creation. Humanity as a whole needs this certainty that God is not up there in the clouds remote and uninvolved. He is actually moving with us through and in the evolutionary process to the final completion of His creation where all will be divinised. The Incarnation was no random event but the point of certainty that what God had begun in the Big Bang He intended finishing along with us and in us. Never again was humanity to wonder whether God existed or if He was unmoved by our struggle to complete our journey.

With courage and conviction Teilhard steps into the breach between traditional theological doctrine and the spirit of St Paul, whose teaching has not been stretched to its prophetic limits. St Paul, as has been said, accepted that the whole of creation is groaning in one great act of giving birth, a perfect description of evolution. But there is yet more analysis of this gestation, St Paul tells us that the work of creation will be complete only when God in Jesus becomes All in All. Teilhard sees this not as Absolute Being existing alongside His creation until its consummation, but being 'fulfilled' *in* His creation through the human nature He has taken to Himself. This would then be not the traditional 'creative causality', (God being the cause of His universe), but 'creative Union', (the deliberate intention of taking on the material of His universe in order to be 'completed' with it). In other words He would not remain separate from His creation but would take full part in its efforts until that time when it would be transformed completely into Him. As Our Lord says to the mystic Vassula Ryden, 'in the end, the whole of creation will come into transforming union of love with Me' (Vassula Ryden, *True Life in God*, vol. 12, p.29).

In Colossians (2:10) St Paul tells us 'In His body lives the fullness of Divinity'. The Jerusalem Bible explains that the word *pleroma* used *by* St Paul here is defined as 'the divinity that is actually *filling* Christ now in His body: that is, the risen Christ, through His Incarnation and Resurrection, unites the Divine and the created. The former is what He is by His pre-existence and His present glory; and the latter is, as human, what He has assumed directly, and, as cosmic, what He assumed indirectly through being human. In this way He is the *pleroma*, or *fullness*, of all possible categories of being' (JB, Col. 2: n. 'e' p.347). Teilhard very bravely postulates that when God the Son became God Incarnate He became something which He had not been before, He became part of His creation, and in this sense God 'changed'.

The Eucharist

As has already been said, for St Gertrude the Sacred Heart of Jesus and the Eucharist are almost synonymous. She easily moves from the delights of one to the delights of the other in the same breath. And again, with Teilhard, just as all the Masses celebrated over time are inseparably One Mass, so the whole universe is the Host which has been 'invaded' and endowed with life through Christ. His Humanity is the material Heart of the universe, His Divinity is the fire which sets the world ablaze through His Heart, transforming it through every Mass when Christ's words are uttered, 'This is My Body'. Those words echo from the beginning of time until the end when all is as it should be, when Christ returns creation 'made new' to His Father.

Through those words 'This is My Body' Christ is present among us Materially and Spiritually, renewing creation through Love.

Christ's Paschal Mystery, or His work of salvation, is manifest in the Mass. At the same time it is inseparable from the Divine eternity, and transcends all times whilst being made present in them all. When Christ descends sacramentally into each one it is in order to join us to Himself physically in a growing world unity (Robert Faricy, *All Things in Christ*, p.28). As our humanity assimilates the material of the world through the Host, and as the Sacred Host assimilates our humanity, step by step it irresistibly invades the universe. As Scripture says, in Christ 'we live, we move, and we are' (Acts 17:28).

The Cross

The Christian idea of a cosmic conflict between good and evil in God's creation is not new but quite ancient. Maximus the Confessor (580–662) describes what took place in Christ's soul in His agony in the Garden of Gethsemane on the night before He died, as the place where the redemption of all creation took place (Hans Urs von Balthasar, *Cosmic Liturgy*, p.271). For Maximus, Christ is the 'cosmic Adam' who unites the whole universe in Himself by His death on the cross. And again, Hugo Rahner in his book *Greek Myths and Christian Mystery* tells us that the 'humble sign of the cross... contains within itself and makes visible all cosmic events, for the nature of all things must be drawn into the drama of redemption through the cross... The outstretched hands of the Logos [Christ], who from the cross embraces the entire world and brings it home to His Father' (Col. 1:20; Hugo Rahner, *Greek Myths and Christian Mystery*, p.51).

Teilhard de Chardin describes this in more apt language. It is the Cross which is the road of universal progress. It is the outcome of the ages through which our conscious endeavours to build a better world, directed and blessed by Christ, are brought back to God. Christ in a real sense is the whole of creation making its way ever upwards to perfection. At the heart of progress is human suffering, rightly accepted and directed, making up for the times creation falls back in its moral development. 'From the very origins of mankind as we know it the Cross was placed on the crest of the road which leads to the highest peaks of creation' (Teilhard de Chardin, *Le Milieu Divin*, p.103–4).

On Good Friday just before his death on Easter Day, 1955, Teilhard wrote to his friend and provincial superior, Father Ravier, regarding the meaning of the Cross: 'What the world is looking for from the Church of God at This Moment: A Generalizing and Deepening of the Meaning of the Cross... the Cross (without losing its expiatory or compensating function) becomes the symbol and the expression of 'evolution' in its fullest sense... And so, without attenuating the Christian tradition, it becomes possible to present to today's world the Cross, not only as a 'consolation' for the world's miseries but as a 'stimulant'... to make progress and to go as far as possible for God... But tomorrow... the crucified God... will become the spiritual mover, the most powerful possible... of ultra-humanization. This is my faith, that I would like to proclaim publicly before I die' (Robert Faricy, *All Things in Christ*, p.81–2).

Science and Religion

The environment of matter is the common universal setting in which we live. It is the womb from whence we come, animate and inanimate alike.

Understanding the universe, however, is unique to humankind, no other species has studied its immediate environment, the world environment and the cosmic environment. No other species has exploited or used for its own development on a worldwide scale the environment of planet Earth. Humankind has within its power – material, intellectual, spiritual – the ability to transform the earth for the benefit of its own species and every species. This is the human prerogative alone (Gen. 1:28–31). And yet Science as a whole has not acknowledged that this is the case. Scientists, with some exceptions, find it difficult to accept that to study the human person in its full perspective requires going beyond investigating human nature only in its biological setting. Instead it is necessary to conduct scientific research from the transcendent experience of people. Every single person has had, however fleetingly, some kind of transcendent experience. To neglect the Spiritual or God element is unreasonable in its fullest sense. Science has indeed given us wonderful new knowledge about ourselves and the universe, but it nevertheless puts 'the block' on understanding our species as more than body, the dimension of the soul is 'out of bounds' as it were. This approach does not accord with our ability to reflect on the whole of our human experience. To deny that many reasonable people, among them scientists, have given good account of the important intellectual questions of our existence which point beyond our earthly reality falls short of a proper scientific approach to the whole of reality (Joseph Ratzinger, *In the Beginning*, p.86).

We are not, as science would have us believe, simply the most highly developed species. The world of non-human creatures is not able to reflect on their own past, present or future. For those species, then, there is no such thing as history in which to situate themselves, there is only instinct to survive. Humankind on the other hand reflects on its past – history therefore is real and has meaning for our present and future. Of all species humankind is *the* 'thinking' species and consequently the most alive. Even though we are unique in this regard, science still behaves as if we are just an anomaly in the evolutionary process. The fact that humankind has displayed developing consciousness throughout its existence, as seen in our ability to continually invent, seems not to be of importance to science, at least, in its effect on the shaping of our planet, let alone the effect it could have on the cosmic system in the future (Teilhard de Chardin, *Man's Place in Nature*, p.35).

Before the Renaissance we had a static view of ourselves and the cosmos, nothing had changed since the creation of the world. As we know, since the nineteenth century this view has been radically changed by science, both our thinking and our beliefs have been challenged. Understanding ourselves to be part of an evolutionary cosmos should not lead us to see ourselves as once having attained the level of *Homo sapiens* we have reached our limit of development and, therefore, our research of the human species can only be retrospective. On the contrary, however, Teilhard says that psychologically humankind has not spoken its last word, as it were, because we are not at this point in time zoologically mature. We have as yet to acknowledge our real future development through our innate drive to total socialisation. We not only have a future, but a 'directed' future through which we move on to an ultra-human plane, or a spiritual plane. Unlike Marxism (not dissimilar to the opinion of science) which believes in achieving one's full potential through the impersonal social organisation of the political system, Christianity believes in the ultimate Person, Christ, Who holds us in existence and takes us into the ultra-personal future (Teilhard de Chardin, *The Future of Man*, p.253).

Since Christ draws His humanity from the Cosmos which He made, it should be natural for there to be reconciliation between Christianity and the pursuit of progress in the world. If our hearts are open to the truth we will see that, throughout history, evolution and progress consist in the always greater organisation of matter resulting in higher levels of spirit.

Progress, then, is a process of spiritualisation which can only be achieved in union with God in and through matter. Humankind's fundamental drive is unification – a process seen in the records of history in the struggle for the rights not only of the oppressed, but of people in general. Human socialisation begets greater consciousness which is the essential ingredient of life development. However, it goes without saying that alongside the spiritualising and humanising value of social unification we experience the dehumanising aspects. In spite of this, though, it is only through the human race's journey towards becoming more and more personalised that we have progressed in our ideas for a better future: building on past knowledge for increased learning; becoming increasingly aware of our responsibility for planning for our immediate human group; then extending this to the wider community, and in the last two centuries, for worldwide society. This has not come about by chance but by the Great Design of God. Without the transcendent pull we cannot, and would not, complete our evolutionary journey because success would be impossible without the convergence of the psychic (or the spiritual) and the physical.

On the other hand, the scientific and Marxist solution finds this belief to be of no relevance to human progress. The best that their solution can offer is an ultra-technified, ultra-socialised, ultra-cerebral future, which will inevitably, as with other species, come to the end of its natural life cycle.

Even though Teilhard's scientific research into the past was a lifelong work, he nevertheless felt it was far more important to ask not how life began but where is it taking us? If we believe universally that individual life extinguishes at biological death, then we believe that the human race has no purposeful future, there is no real motive for development of our race in any direction because, as individuals and as a race, we have no intrinsic value.

Teilhard believed that this would not only be a betrayal of our power of reflection, but also it would mean contradicting ourselves biologically, cutting us off from our natural evolution towards a higher humanity and our arrival at our trans-human destination at the ultimate Heart of things. This contradiction he calls 'dissipation' – a way of describing the lifespan of a species which ends in disintegration and death. On the other hand, 'maturation' of the human species means irreversible development because we are a 'thinking species'. It means a rebirth outside time and space, which is none other than the perfecting of each person's distinctive characteristics through unification of humankind in God. We all share in this heightening of consciousness, but most effectively if we understand these new concepts of matter and new dimensions of cosmic reality. It is noticeable that we are more and more thinking collectively, but ultimate wholeness demands that love of one another be at the centre of our thinking. As a unified whole, humankind has a future, and not just in terms of successive years, but of higher states of consciousness brought about by the struggle we experience to purify our intentions to work for the fulfilment of all.

More thoughts on the phenomenon of Reflection
Throughout the whole evolution of the vertebrate species, including the primate species, only humankind breaks the barrier of reflection. Only humankind develops the consciousness required to move from a simple, instinctive existence to one of complex thought and awareness of past, present and future. In the last two million years numerous species have become extinct, but not one new species has made an appearance on

our planet. As the human group developed its social character and its drive to unification as it migrated to every part of the world, so our thought processes coalesced forming a sphere of thought, along with the biosphere, around the earth.

The process of cerebration within the human species is still going on. Our powers of reflection are becoming more and more global: a species thinking more and more responsibly about the situations of the other. This collective reflection runs co-extensive with the bad behaviour of some and, in spite of it, takes us forward to higher levels of awareness of ourselves as a species. Biologically we are made of the same stuff as other animals but psychically we have left them behind and have gone beyond into the realm of the transcendent. If we care to see it, we can recognise our future progress towards the ultra human, or to put it another way, our evolution from earthbound creatures to transformed, divinised human beings prepared for the dimension of eternity. (Man's place in nature, *see below*,'Unitive Transformation').

Some thoughts on Matter

God created matter – the substance from which all that exists in the dimension of time emerges. In itself matter is unlike God, Who is Spirit. However, God is Unity and it is His nature to unite what He creates. Whatever in creation does not finally enter spiritually into God will either be consigned to eternal disintegration, as with persons, or, will wear out like a garment, as with inanimate matter, and simply cease to be. As the millennia pass there is that which is 'left behind' and that which is ascending to union with God. As for ourselves, our biological substance wears out and we die, but if it has been our desire to become one with God then our soul will live on into eternity and the material side of our nature will decompose until the day of Resurrection when our earthly bodies will be transfigured and reunited with our soul. Mgr de Solages, a friend and defender of Teilhard, in support of Teilhard's position argues that 'since everything in the universe evolved, the thoughts of men evolved with it, and that the problem for theology was how to maintain transcendent values in the midst of this perpetual flux. Truth was immutable, but its expression changed' and 'evolution itself can only be finalistic, that it is advancing towards the spirit, that it can be explained only by the spirit, and that it postulates at the beginning because it postulates at the end, a transcendent God'. (Robert Speaight, *Teilhard de Chardin: A Biography*, p.278)

Unitive Transformation

We live in the presence of God, Who is everywhere (omnipresent). This is not a static presence but a dynamic presence of action through all time and in all places. God has put into every human heart the aspiration to seek Him, and by seeking Him, we might share in His Being – this is called the gift of 'participated being' (Ps. 82:6; John 10:34–5). He so transforms our nature that we become one complex thing with Him (Teilhard de Chardin, *Le Milieu Divin*, p.122). St Paul and St John tell us that it is the action of God making all things new, the mysterious pleroma, or the final completion of all things in which the eternal God and created nature fuse together without confusion into One whilst retaining their own distinctiveness. This action of God does not add anything to Him, in the sense that He lacks anything to make Him whole because 'there was never a time when He was not', but in this sense, that we complete Him only because He became Man that we might become god, that is, one Body one Spirit in Christ (St Athanasius, d.373). God's existence is a unitive existence. The force of Christ's attraction, the truth of His teaching, the power of His grace to change people, inexorably unite us and us in Him through our endeavours to be like Him. We read in Scripture, the saving work of Christ is the unification of all flesh in the one and the same Spirit (Rev. 21:1–7, Eph. 4:9–15, John 3:6, 17).

Related notes on Unitive Transformation
In his first Easter homily Pope Benedict explained:

> Christ's Resurrection... if we may borrow the language of the theory of evolution... is the greatest 'mutation', absolutely the most crucial leap into a totally new dimension that there has ever been in the long history of life and its development: a leap into a completely new order that does concern us, and concerns the whole of history... It is a qualitative leap in the history of 'evolution' and of life in general toward a new future life, toward a new world, which, starting from Christ, already continuously permeates this world of ours, transforms it, and draws it to itself. (S.O. Horn and S. Wiedenhofer, *Creation and Evolution*, p.105)

Cardinal Schonbourn commenting on Pope Benedict's reflection says:

> If the Resurrection of Christ is, so to speak, 'the greatest mutation'... then we may also say: Here is the destination 'of evolution'. Seen from its conclusion and accomplishment, its meaning also becomes manifest. Although in its individual steps it may seem aimless and without direction, the long way did have a meaning when viewed from the perspective of Easter. It is not that the way is

the goal; rather, the Resurrection is the meaning of the way. (S.O. Horn and S. Wiedenhofer, *Creation and Evolution*, p.105)

Pope Francis in his catechesis at his General Audience teaches:

The whole divine Revelation is the fruit of dialogue between God and His People, and faith in the Resurrection is also connected to this dialogue, which supports the journey of God's People in history. It is not astonishing that such a great, such a decisive, such a superhuman mystery as that of the Resurrection required all the itinerary, all the necessary time up to Jesus Christ. He could say: 'I am the resurrection and the life' (John 11:25), because not only is this mystery revealed fully in Him, but it is acted, happens, becomes for the first time a definitive reality. The Gospel we heard, which unites – according to Mark's writing – the account of the Death of Jesus and that of the empty tomb, represents the culmination of that whole journey: it is the event of the Resurrection, which responds to the long search of the People of God, the search of every man and of the whole of humanity.

The Jerusalem Bible in its explanatory note on Ephesians 4:10, 'The One who rose higher than all the heavens to fill all things', comments, 'By ascending through all the cosmic spheres and taking possession of them all one after the other, Christ becomes the Head of the whole *pleroma* or total cosmos, and makes the entire universe acknowledge Him as "Lord".' (JB, p.335, n. 'g')

Consummation

The consummation of the universe requires our co-operation, as willed by God. Teilhard's great prophetic call is driven by this vision, a world taking responsibility for its own destination, its own fulfilment. This requires responding to God's call for our conversion to Him, and it takes the form of a Christian ethics of building towards the future; to deliberately involve oneself in the world in the direction of God's plan to reconcile all things in Christ. Teilhard formulates an ethics in the light of the ultimate future, in the light of the end of the world, the Second Coming of Christ, and the beginning of the world to come. The *Second Coming* will be at the terminal point of human evolution... a transformation of all things in Christ so that God will be 'All in All' (Robert Faricy, *All Things in Christ*, pp.55–6). Teilhard's ethic of building towards the future is the ethic of the Gospel of Love, which teaches us that, through our sacrificial efforts in communion with God, all things will be made new. As Pope Benedict remarks, 'Every explanation of reality that cannot at the same time provide a meaningful and comprehensible view of ethics necessarily remains inadequate', because at the heart of a true ethics there must be reason and love: 'the true reason is love, and love is the true reason', both of which form the two pillars of reality (S.O. Horn and S. Wiedenhofer, *Creation and Evolution*, p.21).

The Second Coming of Christ, or the *Parousia*, will not be identified by change, but will happen suddenly through Divine intervention alone. Nevertheless, there will be a natural continuity from our earthly reality into eternity. Just as now, when an individual dies, there is a transition from his or her human existence to the dimension of life without end. Every endeavour that has been made for human progress in time will not be wasted because this has permanent value in itself. It is not only spiritual progress which counts, but genuine material progress which has worked for the ultimate good of the race and which essentially is the vehicle for the spiritual transformation of creation. As Jesus tells St Gertrude, 'if I took pleasure in spiritual exercises only, surely I would have so reformed human nature after the Fall that there would no longer be any need for either food or clothing...' (Gertrude of Helfta, *The Herald of Divine Love*, p.231). God in His providence brings about the death of each one of us at a moment which not only directs the destiny of the individual soul, but in its own obscure way progresses the whole of creation to its completion.

A theological understanding of creation is explained as God's continuous creation to the *pleroma,* and we are God's living extension of His creative power, and sharers in its unfolding. Christ puts it thus in the book *I Am With You*: 'The presence in you of My Spirit means that in your life is enacted something of the universal conflict present in My creation. See the ultimate victory in creation of My cause as that which is possible in your own life. This will help you see all that is of darkness as conquerable – and destined, in you, to be put to flight... just so surely as it will be within My universe' (Fr John Woolley, *I Am with You*, p.157). This is not only a theological understanding of creation but an organic understanding because God transcending time, by His action, influences the present and the future with us and for us.

Teilhard's image of the end of the world

The transformation of our race will result in a mature union of consciousness. Nevertheless, to decide for God will be an individual and fully human act. The universal Christ will receive our decision, and there will be an inevitable schism between those souls who cannot accept an existence of union in the dimension of eternity and those who choose to live an eternal communion in God. Those who reject the irreversible history and destination of the world in God will enter a never-ending existence of spiritual decomposition. Those who choose Union in its as yet unimaginable beauty will enter into life eternal where the Amazing Adventure of the spiritualising of creation will be seen in its perfection, and experienced as utterly satisfying to our human nature, now become divinised.

Christ Omega two thousand years ago told the Apostles at the Last Supper, 'I have many things to say to you but they would be too much for you now. But when the Spirit of Truth comes He will lead you to the complete truth' (John 16:12–13). Teilhard de Chardin's unshakeable belief in the future convinced him that 'ours' is the time in which the Holy Spirit is leading us to understand the truth (to be thrilled by it and not to shrink from it) which is God's amazing Enterprise for His Creation in union with Jesus Christ, Our Lord. Amen

'The Face of Everyman:

Christ yesterday and today, the beginning and the end, Alpha and Omega, all time belongs to Him, and all the ages, to Him be glory and power, through every age and for ever.

(Easter Vigil)

THE FACE OF EVERYMAN:
Christ Jesus Our Lord

And we, with our unveiled faces reflecting like mirrors the brightness of the Lord all grow brighter and brighter as we are turned into the image that we reflect; this is the work of the Lord who is Spirit. (2 Cor. 3:18)

Preamble

There are those in life whose God-given task it is to prophesy, to see to the heart of the value and purpose of human existence. The cosmos, as wonderful as it is, is still a tapestry in progress. The work yet to do is to understand the 'within' of the universe. We do this through the Spirit, whose Presence in Creation can only be seen by eyes which are in harmony with the desires of God, and through hearts which are open to the revelation of God present in the whole of His Creation, material and spiritual.

In my last little work, 'Christ Omega', I outlined Teilhard de Chardin's prophetic vision reflecting St Paul's thought with regard to the consummation of the Universe in Christ. In this work I am making an attempt at outlining (based on Teilhard's *Hymn of the Universe*) the specific way in which God brings this about, that is, by transforming material reality from within. He takes matter in which the Spirit is present, but not recognised, and transforms it so that the Spirit can be seen blazing forth. The Spirit reshapes our outward appearance only in so far as He is allowed by us, as free persons, to enable our inner reality to shine through.

Less sophisticated peoples quite naturally saw themselves as part of the 'within' of the universe, worshipping God, with one's whole person, body and soul, heart and mind. Creation is good and God is restoring it and healing it, making His world whole. In their daily lives there was no barrier between earth and heaven because God penetrates, informs and consecrates the temporal order. The temporal order carries a deeper sense of mystery, a sense of what lies beyond (Esther de Waal (Ed.), *The Celtic Vision*, pp.5–14)

Our generation has lost this vision and consequently the will to view our earthly existence as a preparation, along with God, for the realisation of the new heavens and the new earth through the Spirit's work of Transforming Union.

Scripture is the heart and soul of God's revelation of His Transforming Spirit, so I have used Scripture, and particularly St Paul's writings, to support Teilhard's understanding.

Introduction

'The Church as the Body of Christ... can be called the fullness (pleroma); ... in so far as it includes the whole new creation that shares (since it forms the setting of the human race) in the cosmic rebirth under Christ its Ruler and Head... The adverbial phrase "All in All" is used to suggest something of limitless size...' (Eph. 1:23; JB, p.331, n. 'u').

The importance of understanding Our Lord's work of Transforming Union for the future of the human race is crucial to our conviction that our work as a race is to become what God intended us to be, and that is, 'One Body, One Spirit in Christ' (Eph. 4:4). That Body is the whole of created matter destined to be Divinised through Christ's transforming work in us. It is also crucial for those in our race who do not see purpose and meaning to life that they be given a vision of what immense hope 'God's call holds for us', what 'rich glories' our work on earth will yield for us if we allow Him to 'enlighten the eyes of our mind' so as to appreciate the tremendous task He has laid out for us to achieve (Eph. 1:18).

The task to be achieved is to work to bring about that Unity of all things with which the whole of existence is endowed, and which is the same as the Unity that exists within God Himself ('Before anything was created, He existed.' Col. 1:17). The unifying power of Christ's very Being means that through His Presence we are inseparably linked together and only exist, in reality, as one Body. The quality of our existence depends on our allowing Christ's Presence to help us understand and live, through time, our primordial bond of solidarity. As the Church teaches, 'Christ is the Lord of the cosmos and of history. In Him human history and indeed all creation are "set forth" and transcendently fulfilled' (CCC n. 668). For Teilhard, accepting the truth of this bond is a question of life or death, because if we do not believe in the sustaining radiance of the Presence of Christ we will surely die of cold (Teilhard de Chardin, *Hymn of the Universe*, p.25).

'Do all you can to preserve the unity of the Spirit by the peace that binds you together. There is one Body, one Spirit, just as you were all called into one and the same hope when you were called. There is one Lord, one faith, one baptism, and one God who is Father all of all, over all, through all, and within all' (Eph. 4:3–6).

Humanity in Formation

'From the beginning till now the entire creation , as we know, has been groaning in one great act of giving birth; and not only creation , but all of us who possess the first-fruits of the Spirit, we too groan inwardly as we wait for our bodies to be set free' (Rom. 8:22–3).

The rebuilding of the spiritual reality of Christ's Body can be likened to a building under construction. The materials of this building are composed of the spiritual soul and materiality itself. The construction consists in the divinisation of both the time and place in which each is born. There is no such thing as 'chance' in the time and place we each come into existence, as each life is destined to be for the world's genuine progress towards its final end. The structure of the building is an organic structure of development through which Christ perfects all our endeavours to build the Kingdom on earth as it is in Heaven. Every part of God's creation is brought into being at the most advantageous time, and only God knows how He can best use every element. It is up to us to co-operate with His plan.

The messages of *True Life in God* make plain to us, in spiritual terms, by the words of Jesus, just how the 'new earth' *is* being laboriously refashioned through His purifying activity and our co-operation:

Allow My Holy Spirit to cultivate your soil and make a terrestrial Eden in you, let My Holy Spirit make a New Earth to prosper in you your soil so that your first earth, that was the devil's property, wears away; then once again My Glory will shine in you and all the divine seeds sown in you by My Spirit will sprout and grow in My divine light... The New Heavens? they too will be inside you, when My Holy Spirit will govern you in holiness. My Holy Spirit, consort of My Throne, will shine in your darkness like a splendid sun in the sky because the Word will be given to you to express thoughts and speech as I would wish you to think and speak – everything expressed will be in accordance with My Image and thought, everything you will do will be to Our likeness because the Spirit of your Father will be speaking in you and your New Universe will march with My Holy Spirit to conquer the rest of the stars (symbolic for 'people'), for My Glory and those who had not observed My Law and were fully drawn away like a passing shadow into darkness, never knowing the hope and holiness I was reserving for your times. (Vassula Ryden, *True Life in God*, bk v, pp.100–101)

When I was a child, I used to talk like a child, and think like a child and argue like a child, but now I am a man, all childish ways are put behind me. (1 Cor. 13:11)

You must want love more than anything else. (1 Cor. 14:1)

Even the most primitive belief in the Divine, seen throughout the duration of the evolutionary process, shows the growing desire through humanity's actions to love and be loved. Not just out of self-interest or self-preservation but genuine self-sacrificing love on behalf of the nuclear family, the extended family, the tribe, the nation and, in our day, the world over. In the final resort each person can only truly find his or her lasting happiness in union with the whole of created beings centred on God. Anything less has proven to be a failure. Not that each of us can love all beings with equal intensity but we can cherish the innate value of each being and the necessity of its existence in the overall scheme of things. Creative Divine transforming love in Christ has no exact parallel in human relationships, except to say that people do experience through their genuinely self-sacrificing relationships, personal development and its effect in others, unlike the retrograde effects of behaviour which only has self-interest at heart.

Biological progress and spiritual progress move forward together. Biological progress depends on spiritual progress for its survival. Biological disintegration comes about by the laws of nature being altered to suit human self-interested desires. Only by seeing the spiritual unity of all things will progress be made because our biological progress and spiritual progress are organically bound to one another. The false ambitions of the world lead to disaster as we see it every day: war and the lust for power, the destruction of the environment through greed, the abuse of our fellow human beings for our own gratification. Unless our thinking and intentions turn from the forces of hate and selfishness towards the unifying forces of love we will continue to descend to ever greater depths of human misery and disintegration. Love achieves where rigid law-making fails because only love can develop the individual at the deepest level, uniting the one with the many: embracing the whole world bringing it biologically and spiritually to completion.

As has been said, our existence comprising created cosmic matter and immortal spirit is, by the grace of God, destined to become 'flesh' of the Incarnate Christ's 'flesh'. The more we throw ourselves into the work of the human enterprise, the more fully will our efforts produce in us our likeness to Christ. Our efforts too will not end with our physical death but, because they have a cosmic purpose, will endure as the building blocks for the transformation of the old earth into the new.

Christ in the world of Matter
'The hidden wisdom of God which we teach in our mysteries is the wisdom that God predestined to be for our

glory before the ages began... we teach what Scripture calls: the things that no eye has seen and no ear heard, things beyond the mind of man, all that God has prepared for those that love Him' (Isa. 64:4; 1 Cor. 2:7–9).

The Heart of the Universe

To help us understand the truth that we are being transformed into the image of Christ according to our efforts to complete the cosmic Body of Christ, Teilhard describes an experience he had whilst praying in a Church before a picture of the Sacred Heart of Jesus. He relates how the Heart of Christ in the picture was universalised as he focused on it, vibrating with His Divine Spirit. Whilst reading it we should see in it an image, if you like, of how our own human material reality, body and spirit, is in essence being transformed, spiritualised, divinised.

As he prayed he was turning certain things over in his mind, and was confused and saddened by the knowledge that if Christ came and stood among us very few would recognise Him as God, even though His Divinity would be shining through His physicality. Preoccupied with this thought he found himself, quite unconsciously, looking at a traditional painting of Christ offering His Heart to His people. Still looking, he continued to turn these things over in his mind, and gradually realised that he was being given a mystical understanding of the Heart of Christ. The outlines of the image of Christ, His face, His clothing, etc. began to fade into the rest of the picture, there seemed to be no dividing lines between the image and that which surrounded it. Everything the image 'touched' became a single vibrant pulsating whole.

The traditional representation of holiness seen as a glow of light (or halo) coming forth from the face and head of Christ spread out into infinity, and at the same time, gave the impression of a bloodstream or nervous system supporting everything that existed. The entire universe was alive through this radiation, but simultaneously all things possessed their own identity. The source of this power seemed to come pre-eminently from the Heart of Christ. But, it was the transfigured face of Christ which enchanted Teilhard most.

Every shade of beauty was to be seen in Christ's face, majestic in its sweetness and tenderness, possessing a harmony which was entirely satisfying to the soul. And yet at the same time above and beyond this experience was the certainty of the intangible, incommunicable beauty of Christ Himself, unifying all the other tangible beauties.

In the eyes of Christ were to be seen mystery and grandeur, at once motherly and passionate, and again noble and masterly, courageous and strong. All of this provoked a response of unspeakable happiness. Nevertheless, within the depths of the eyes was an indistinguishable expression both of great agony and unconquerable joy (Teilhard de Chardin, *Hymn of the Universe*, pp.42–6)

Eucharist – Transforming Love
On another occasion Teilhard was given to understand the way in which that other great reality of Christ's Real Presence in the universe, His Body, Blood, Soul and Divinity, which we receive through the Sacred Host in Holy Communion, exerts its influences on the destiny of physical existence.

As he prayed in front of the Sacred Host in the monstrance on the altar, the host began rapidly to expand and radiate light. At first he had little or no reaction until it grew so large that it became very near to him. He heard a barely audible sound which resembled a yearning or deep longing as the tide of whiteness enwrapped everything. The whiteness did not alter those things which it enveloped but left them as they were, as they had been created, but nevertheless, invaded them in the centre of their being, at a depth which could not be sounded. The universe was glowing from within and everything was made of the same translucent substance.

The dark world had gone and was now a great white host. It seemed that at this point the cosmos had reached its amplitude, but this was not so. Within the substance of things purifying activity was taking place. What was purified became one with this deep intense light. The purification gathered into one every power to love, making whole all things from within, liberating the attachments of the heart and will and gathering into itself all that is pure love, moulding these with exuberance within its vigorous light.

As the host folded in on itself those elements in the universe not purified remained outside in the blackness. Their glow now was not the living light of God, but the cancerous light of rebellion (Teilhard de Chardin, *Hymn of the Universe*, pp.47–9; Matt. 25:46).

The Presence of the Spirit in Matter

These are the very things that God has revealed to us through the Spirit, for the Spirit reaches the depths of everything, even the depths of God (1 Cor. 2:10).

Since the beginning of time the Holy Spirit has been present in the matter of the cosmos:

In the beginning God created the heavens and the earth. Now the earth was a formless void, there was darkness over the deep, and God's Spirit hovered over the water. (Gen. 1:1–2)

53

You give breath, fresh life begins, you keep renewing the world. (Ps. 104:30)

The Spirit of God is the source of all being and life. (Ps. 104:30; JB, p.888, n. 'f')

The Spirit of the Lord, indeed, fills the whole world, and that which holds all things together knows every word that is said. (Wisd, 1:7)

Teilhard's fundamental belief that the spiritual increases with the development of 'thinking life', as part of the evolutionary process, is the context in which he situates his understanding of the recreation of the 'new heavens and the new earth'.

The story of evolution unfolds for us the story of the revelation of the Spirit in matter. Throughout the journey of humankind's development, the Spirit has manifested Himself ever more clearly to our understanding through the dimension of thought. As our ability to reason progressed, so did our knowledge of God and His Revelation of Himself by the Spirit become clear, particularly through Scripture:

Small blame, however, attaches to these men, for perhaps they only go astray in their search for God and their eagerness to find Him; living among His works, they strive to comprehend them and fall victim to appearances, seeing so much beauty. Even so, they are not to be excused: if they are capable of acquiring enough knowledge to be able to investigate the world, how have they been so slow to find its Master? (Wisd. 13:6–9)

It is the Creator of the world, ordaining the process of man's birth and presiding over the origin of all things, who in His mercy will most surely give you back both breath and life… (2 Macc. 7:23)

Since the God who made the world and everything in it is Himself Lord of heaven and earth, He does not make His home in shrines made by human hands. Nor is He dependent on anything; on the contrary, it is He who gives everything – including life and breath – to every-one. (Acts 17:24–6).

For what can be known about God is perfectly plain to them since God Himself has made it plain. Ever since God created the world, His everlasting power and deity – however invisible – have been there for the mind to see in the things He has made. (Rom. 1:19–20)

The more we focus on the biological origins of our existence in isolation from the spiritual, the less we understand our destiny. To uncover our future we must discover that our full develop-ment and its purpose are inseparable from the evolutionary process. In our efforts to prove a natural emergence of life in order to dispel the myth that we have a supernatural beginning we are led down false byways and away from the full beauty of what it means to be a body-soul reality; a spiritual being coming more alive as we live in tune with our true nature – the wonder of the flower is revealed not in its shoot but in its full bloom. Science does humanity a grave injury when it studies the material reality of the person only, resisting the obvious that there is far more to investigate 'within' the human person (Teilhard de Chardin, *Hymn of the Universe*, pp.77–8).

We most certainly are burying our head in the sand when we ignore the evidence of humanity's gradual recognition of the transcendent side of our nature. God's dealings with us on a personal level and as a race became more and more part of our lived experience. God as Creator, or the 'Power' greater than the human race, was over time revealed as a 'Someone' for us to interact with and not simply a 'force' which controls us.

> God said, 'Here is the sign of the Covenant I make between Myself and you and every living creature with you for all generations. I set My bow in the clouds and it shall be a sign of the Covenant between Me and the earth. (Gen. 9:12–13)

> Yahweh said to Abram, 'Leave your country, your family and your father's house, for the land I will show you. I will make you a great nation; I will bless you and make your name so famous that it will be used as a blessing. (Gen. 12:1–2)

> Yahweh spoke to Moses, He said: 'Speak to the whole community of the sons of Israel and say to them: "Be holy, for I, Yahweh your God, am Holy".' (Lev. 19:2)

When Christ entered the pattern of history it was the point of certainty for those who witnessed it and for every generation which follows. This Revelation through the Spirit was not partial. What was seen in Christ was the true nature of the moving force in creation – 'with the all-important truth that everything is *love-inspired*' (Fr John Woolley, *I Am With You*, pp.32/134).

He is the One that (even those who do not believe but are

searching the cosmos for answers) must be found personally if their searching is to bear lasting fruit in certainty, because that is the gift of enquiry that God has given each of us 'to seek and find Him' (Jer. 29:13) in a personal relationship. Then the knowledge of the cosmos and its 'secrets' will become clear and make perfect sense since in that relationship our present existence and our future existence will take on compelling meaning and draw us into action to help build the new earth.

The grandeur of our existence is to be found in the spiritual nature of our being which reveals to us the inextricable part the natural world plays in the process of becoming One Body One Spirit in Christ (The Mass, Eucharistic Prayer III). God's creative act is one single activity: Christ's saving work, His Life, Death and Resurrection in the evolutionary process although separated in time from the initial creation is a single work of Unity, they cannot be separated; they are ONE. Through the Spirit, Grace entered the world at the moment of creation, carrying out its work throughout time. At the point when human persons entered the world they were endowed with this same Grace, giving them the capacity of coming to know the Divine. Their nature was at once physical and transcendent. Our human nature, as individuals or as a race, could not develop towards its likeness to the Divine without its 'natural ingredients' of matter and spirit (Gen. 2:7). In no other way was it possible to become supremely real without the influence of the Spirit of Grace on the stuff of our nature. All other animal species are not personal, transcendent or free and therefore do not have the capacity for self-development.

It was Christ's Incarnation 'planned' from all eternity which prepared and directed the developments which have taken place since the beginning of the evolutionary cycle. It is Christ's Incarnation which breathes accelerated thinking life into the universe – pre-eminently in the moral sphere. Human development in all areas of life has at its foundation the moral directive. All progress proceeds or collapses depending on how moral principles are applied and lived. We not only see this but experience it in our personal lives, as well as in human achievement. We alone are endowed with intelligence sufficient to change the world for the better. That is why every effort, no matter how material, if carried out from the pure intention of building up the Body of Christ, has a positive effect, not only for contemporary society but for the future of the race. An evolution which is only material in basis would leave no room for thinking man, whose nature is spiritual, because this spiritual nature is given to us for the purpose of playing our part in the divinisation of nature.

John also declared, 'I saw the Spirit coming down from heaven like a dove and resting on Him, I did not know Him myself, but He who sent me to baptise with water had said to me, "The man on whom you see the Spirit come down and rest is the One who is going to baptise with the Holy Spirit."' (John 1:32–4)

Nicodemus said, 'How can a grown man be born? Can he go back into his mother's womb and be born again?' Jesus replied: 'I tell you solemnly, unless a man is born through water and the Spirit, he cannot enter the kingdom of God.' (John 3:4–6)

…the water that I shall give will turn into a spring inside him, welling up to eternal life. (John 4:14)

…when the Spirit of Truth comes He will lead you to the complete truth. (John 16:13)

> These are the very things God has revealed to us through
> the Spirit, for the Spirit reaches the depths of everything,
> even the depths of God. (1 Cor. 2:10, 11)

There are, and always have been 'seers' who experience the
Presence of the Spirit within matter, who have been shown the
'within' of material existence. These mystics God has given to
the rest of humanity so that they can teach us the reality of the
Presence of the Spirit within matter, and what this means for
humanity's future. As we work towards that for which we were
created, that is, a union of participated being in the life of God
(or 'gods by participation') (Ps. 82:6; John 10:34–5) we see this
in a veiled but real way through the experiences of our daily
lives. Works of art down the centuries have depicted those who
have tried to live a God-centred life by showing their subjects
surrounded by an aureole of light (or in common parlance,
a halo). This is something that artists and other people have
recognised as the Spirit shining through physicality, revealing
our true nature as a body-soul reality.

> And after the fire there came the sound of a gentle breeze.
> And when Elijah heard this, he covered his face with his
> cloak and went out and stood at the entrance of the cave
> (1 Kgs 19:13) ('The whisper of a light breeze signifies
> that God is a spirit and that he converses intimately with
> His prophets.' JB, p.447, n. 19 'e').
>
> The hand of Yahweh was laid on me, and He carried
> me away by the Spirit of Yahweh and set me down in the
> middle of a valley, a valley full of dried bones. … He said
> to me, 'Son of man, can these bones live?' I said, 'You
> know, Lord Yahweh.' He said prophesy over these bones.
> Say, 'Dry bones, hear the word of Yahweh…'. He said

to me, 'Prophesy to the breath; ... say to the breath, "The Lord Yahweh says this: Come from the four winds, breath; breathe on these bones; let them live...".' (Ezek 37:1–10)

... He took with Him Peter and John and James and went up the mountain to pray. As He prayed, the aspect of His face changed and His clothing became brilliant as lightning. Suddenly there were two men there talking to Him; they were Moses and Elijah appearing in glory, and they were speaking of His passing which He was to accomplish in Jerusalem. (Luke 9:28–31)

But I will move on to visions and revelations I have had from the Lord. I know a man in Christ who, fourteen years ago, was caught up – whether still in the body or out of the body, I do not know, God knows... was caught up into paradise and heard things which must not and cannot be put into human language. (2 Cor. 12:1–4)

My name is John, and through our union in Jesus I am your brother and share your sufferings, your kingdom, and all you endure: I was on the island of Patmos for having preached God's word and witnessed for Jesus; it was the Lord's day and the Spirit possessed me, and I heard a voice behind me, shouting like a trumpet, 'Write down all that you see in a book, and send it to the seven Churches...'. (Rev. 1:9–11)

When you showed me your most longed-for face, full of blessedness, as I have just said, so close to mine (though I am so undeserving), I felt as though an ineffable light from your Divine eyes were entering through my eyes, softly penetrating, passing through all my interior being, in a way beyond measure, wonderful, working with marvellous power in every limb. At first it was as though my bones were being emptied of all the marrow, then even the bones with the flesh were dissolved so that nothing was left to exist in all my substance save that Divine splendour which in a manner more delectable than I am able to say, playing within itself, showed my soul the inestimable bliss of utter serenity. (Gertrude of Helfta, *The Herald of Divine Love*, pp.125–6; Vassula Ryden, *True Life In God*, VII notebooks 84–94, p.84ff.)

Our spirit is indestructible. It can only take us in the direction of immortality and hence fulfilment. Spirit will remain when all else has disappeared and has been transformed. Otherwise there would be no universal ambition to strive together to attain our goal; why should we strive, if there is no prospect of attainment of ultimate union in a life of blessedness? If we did not have faith that this is God's design, it would be difficult to respect the phenomenon of the rational human person and our immortal nature. The fact that the human race alone reflects (and more and more collectively) on the nature and purpose of the world means that reflection has had, and still does have, a bearing in the development of the evolutionary journey.

Now we are seeing a dim reflection in a mirror; but then we shall be seeing face to face. The knowledge that I have now is imperfect; but then I shall know as fully as I am known. (1 Cor. 13:12–13)

For us, our homeland is in heaven, and from heaven comes the Saviour we are waiting for, the Lord Jesus Christ, and He will transfigure these wretched bodies of ours into copies of His Glorious Body. He will do that by the same power with which He can subdue the whole universe. (Phil. 3:20–21)

Prayer, vehicle of Transforming Spirit

The Spirit too comes to help us in our weakness. For
when we cannot choose words in order to pray properly,
the Spirit Himself expresses our plea in a way that could
never be put into words, and God who knows everything
in our hearts knows perfectly well what He means, and
that the pleas of the saints expressed by the Spirit are
according to the mind of God. (Rom. 8:26–7)

At the heart of our transformation is dialogue with God and
the acceptance of his infallible influence in our lives. The Holy
Spirit is the Person whose intimate knowledge of our interior
selves guides and directs our prayer. Teilhard, believing
wholeheartedly in the efficacy of prayer, remained faithful to
his relationship with God and the world. He steadfastly prayed
his way through his work and personal life. He intended to
do his utmost to be a vehicle through which the universe and
each individual could be recreated through Love. As far as he
was concerned, choosing to play a full part in the consummation of the Body of Christ was not an option, but a duty, not
only to God, but to the human race for its ultimate fulfilment.
Every living being has a very real influence, for the most part
unwittingly, on the universe around him or her, for good or
ill, according to the positive development of each person's
personality. Prayer, or talking with God, is the human person's
God-given way of developing our closeness to Him. Teilhard
believed that the 'single soul' of humanity could only come
about by practising love in all its aspects. We awaken the spirit
in the world by allowing Christ to work on us in such a way
that He transforms our thinking, speaking and acting until we
become 'flesh of His flesh and bone of His bone' (Gen. 2:23)
'…and I live not now with my own life but with the life of

Christ who lives in me' (Gal. 2:20) ('The living acts of the Christian somehow become the acts of Christ.' JB, Ch. 21, p.325, n. 'm'). Christ unites in Himself the vastness of creation and our small being, and with Him we engage in the battle for the coming of the new heavens and new earth ('The presence, in you, of My Spirit, means that in your life is enacted something of the universal conflict present in My creation… See the ultimate victory, in creation, of My cause as that which is possible in your own life. This will help you see all that is of darkness as conquerable – and destined, in you, to be put to flight… just as surely as it will within My universe.' Fr John Woolley, *I Am With You*, p.157).

Out of His infinite glory, may He give you the power through His Spirit for your hidden self to grow strong, so that Christ may live in your hearts through faith, and then, planted in love and built on love, you will with all the saints have strength to grasp the breadth and the length, the height and the depth; until, knowing the love of Christ, which is beyond all knowledge, you are filled with the utter fullness of God. (Eph. 3:16–19)

There is, though, a resistance in us to block the transforming grace we receive in the Sacraments, and especially the Eucharist, because of our freedom of will. Teilhard views this as our remaining in darkness, refusing to allow the universe to 'move on' since each is inextricably immersed in it; refusing to allow all those necessary virtues and qualities of life to blossom: courage, enterprise, holiness, appreciation of God. We stunt our growth and that of the whole world by restricting the flow of Divine Life. On the other hand, if we open ourselves to Christ's influence we become a creative spur in the Body of Christ. The Spirit of Christ is ever more present to us in every determined, selfless act, in every acceptance of God's will in our lives, be that in the enjoyment of life's good things or giving all in the service of God for His Greater Glory.

> Glory be to Him whose power, working in us, can do infinitely more than we can ask or imagine… (Eph. 3:20)

Teilhard saw the reflection of Our Lady's creative power in the beauty of her purity and prayer which carried Her along on the path of truly blessed service for the furtherance of Christ's Body.

Christianity, an upward-lifting and unifying force at the heart of human endeavour

Having a crystal clear understanding that Christians are imperfect in love, Teilhard, nevertheless, believed implicitly that the Church is the axis through which her members strive through everyday living to establish on earth God's Kingdom of justice, love and peace, because we each in our own way are called to love perfectly, just as God loves perfectly ('You must be perfect just as your heavenly Father is perfect.' Matt. 5:48). ('It is because love is the mainspring of all phenomena that it is always challenged by evil. When love can be destroyed, evil is satisfied… The collapse of love is always life's foremost tragedy; it means that everything planned for human satisfaction and soul-progress is halted.' Fr John Woolley, *I Am With You*, p.179).

Human progress and the Kingdom of God do not contradict one another; in fact they are two sides of the same coin. Without the goal of the Kingdom human progress will end up going nowhere. Without the effort to perfect human progress the Kingdom will not come to perfection on earth. There is no reason to become perfect if there is not an Infinitely Perfect Being calling us into the future to share His life. ('...where a man sows, there he reaps: if he sows in the field of self-indulgence he will get a harvest of corruption out of it; if he sows in the field of the Spirit he will get from it a harvest of eternal life.' Gal. 6:7–9)

The Church on earth is endowed already with a sanctity that is real though imperfect. In Her members perfect holiness is something yet to be acquired. (CCC n. 825) ('It is necessary that temptations come...' Matt. 18:7)

Because they are members of the Body whose Head is Christ, Christians contribute to building up the Church by the constancy of their convictions and their moral lives. The Church increases, grows and develops through the holiness of her faithful, until 'we all attain to the unity of the faith and of the knowledge of the Son of God, to mature manhood, to the measure of the stature of the fullness of Christ...' (CCC n. 2045)

By living with the mind of Christ, Christians hasten the coming of the Reign of God, 'a kingdom of justice, love and peace.' They do not, for all that, abandon their earthly tasks; faithful to their Master, they fulfil them with uprightness, patience and love... (CCC n. 2046)

Given humankind's historic struggle in the fight for progress as opposed to stagnation or disintegration, Teilhard reflects that the inevitability of the appearance of sin has to be accepted, but this does not mean we can identify or pinpoint a definite historical moment in place or time (CCC n. 390). And the fact that sin has contaminated the whole race (apart from Our Lady who was conceived without sin but born into a contaminated world (CCC n. 1869)) must be accepted, since our life's experience verifies this – none of us can contradict that. The mention earlier of God's grace being totally appropriate for time and place in our spiritual evolution applies directly to our sinful nature. Teilhard believed firmly in the grace of Baptism as the source of God's life which is necessary for the recreation of the person. This grace cannot be anything other than an eternal grace since God Himself is eternal, but its effect depends on our response to the Spirit's promptings at any point in our lives to grow in the love of God and neighbour if we are to do our duty for the redemption of the world ('Healing the wounds of sin, the Holy Spirit renews us interiorly through a spiritual transformation. He enlightens and strengthens us to live as "children of light" through "all that is good and right and true".' CCC n. 1695; 'The forms and tasks of life are many but holiness is one…' LG, 41).

Love of a Greater Being has never been absent from the human race. Mystics and ordinary people alike in every civilisation and religion have embraced belief in a Supreme Deity – this is not a specifically Christian phenomenon by any means. Since love of God and His influence are experienced and expressed from one era to the next it is not expected that humanism or some form of belief in earthly values will replace love of God and of neighbour as a way forward. Christianity has all that is needed to make a 'success' of the human race's mission. All other religions and secular efforts God uses to complete His Plan (Teilhard de Chardin, *Hymn of the Universe*, pp.154–5)

Straining ahead – Christian Ambition for the completion of Christ Omega

I strain ahead for what is still to come; I am racing for the finish for the prize to which God calls us upwards to receive in Christ Jesus. (Phil. 3:14)

Since God holds every single aspect or element of His creation in being (even those beings who reject Him), it is vital that those of us who do not reject Him offer the world the treasures God is offering us.

The Christian Church offers these treasures which give total meaning to the universe. They are what is needed for maximum coherence of our intellect and maximum impetus for our action. It is the religion of progress because it teaches humanity's relationship to the cosmos and its reason for existence.

Firstly evolution and Christianity coincide – both are moving in the direction of higher states of consciousness and spirituality. The universe is the biological home within which humanity is born and dies. Therefore, it is the natural environment in which the spiritual nature of each person develops and grows according to the awareness of each and the desire of each for their spiritual fulfilment, or the soul's satisfaction. There is a disharmony in our daily lives when either the biological or spiritual dominate our activity. The Christian does not have to annihilate his or her body but saves body and soul for the Resurrection.

Teilhard believed passionately that every stage in a person's life was an integral stage for completing the Body of Christ. Each stage had to be lived to the full in whatever possible way this could be achieved. He believed that no effort is wasted, every effort is an act of love which transforms the individual and completes the whole, and none more so than the deliberate effort in preparing for death. ('I have fought the good fight to the end; I have run the race to the finish; I have kept the faith; all there is to come now is the crown of righteousness reserved for me, which the Lord, the righteous Judge will give to me on that Day; and not only to me but to all those who have longed for His Appearing.' 2 Tim. 4:7–8)

Even the limitations of later life should not prevent us from seeing our ambitions fulfilled. Every stage has potential for personal growth: enfeeblement, loneliness – each of these is an opportunity for transformation through the Spirit. A youthful, happy attitude is perfectly possible. Accepting one's state at the end of life is living to the full. There is as much to achieve for the creation of the world when one is in his or her declining years as there is when one is young. Christ gave us every stage of life and through these stages we make, because of our right motive, a valuable contribution to the process of the development of life, and this is so even in death. Teilhard saw that the work to be done is more enduring than the earthly life of the individual when death comes. The work which each person has completed in love for the furtherance of the universe will be left intact. You could say another layer of the building will be firmly in place. Moreover the time of death of each renders its own fruitfulness for itself and for the completion of creation ('The life and death of each of us has its influence on others...' Rom. 14:7–8). There will be continuity of love and endeavour in the dimension of eternity for every soul, along with the knowledge that our efforts have been cemented in that reality greater than ourselves, and yet which would not have been so if we had not played our part. ('My child, it is the sense of future which gives the element of thrill to a growing relationship with Myself... Even with the passing years, every interest every ambition can still be a cause for enthusiasm. This, to the unbeliever, may seem illogical, but where a life has Me as its foundation, there is an awareness that whatever worthwhile is undertaken, carries with it a sense of permanence. The amount of time left in a life does not matter... because whatever is begun, at any stage, will be seen as part of a continuing process.' Fr John Woolley, *I Am with You*, p.147)

The necessity of human endeavour for the completion of the Body of Christ

Teilhard's concern for 'God's project' to come to fulfilment was completely selfless. He endeavoured to 'spend himself' in this work, but did not see it as 'his' achievement as such, but the achievement of the whole race. He saw God's plan of Transforming Union, and the human race's part in it, as an irresistible invitation to complete, with God, the work of Creation. God has conferred on His children the amazing dignity of working alongside Him to complete the Mystical Body of Christ. Teilhard taught unambiguously that from God alone and not otherwise can we receive the power to be reformed to the image and likeness of our original state ('Let us make man in our own Image, in the Image of Ourselves let us make him.' Gen. 1:26). ('Human activity proceeds from man: it is also ordered to him. When he works, not only does he transform matter and society, but fulfils himself... in accordance with God's will and design... to enable men as individuals and as members of society to pursue and fulfil their total vocation.' *Gaudium et Spes*, Ch. III, n. 35)

The Presence of the Spirit of Love gives meaning to possibilities far more effectively than our independent efforts to achieve because having taken God into our lives we are automatically united with His victory. The light of God's love surrounding us and the light of His power within us to act are one whole.

As a scientist and a priest, Teilhard set out to help others appreciate that the evolutionary plan of God and our essential part in it liberates us to work for the increase of Divine life within ourselves and the universe ('…what is man that You should care for him… you have crowned him with glory and splendour, made him lord over the work of your hands, set all things under his feet.' Ps. 8:4–6). He believed that humankind was created to investigate and manipulate our environment for the wellbeing and furtherance of the race, even to a hundred-fold, for the glory of God ('And the one who received the seed in rich soil is the man who hears the word and understands it; he is the one who yields a harvest and produces now a hundredfold…' Matt. 13:23). He desired that we recognise the indwelling of the Spirit in the total harmony and indescribable beauty of our universe which glows with God's splendour ('the heavens proclaim the glory of God, the vault of heaven proclaims His handiwork…' Ps. 19:1). The fundamental issue for Teilhard was our work for the realisation of the Kingdom ('Thy Kingdom come, Thy Will be done on earth as it is in Heaven' … 'The Kingdom of God is within you.' Luke 17:21).

The Universe as the Way of the Soul's Fulfilment

It is only with Me – your life's goal fixed – that you can notice the fashioning of steps towards Myself out of what would seem utterly pointless and barren. Those who do not know Me cannot see My ordaining of the world as the way of the soul's fulfilment. (Fr John Woolley, *I Am with You*, p.177)

There was always the steadfast conviction in Teilhard's understanding of the universe and its purpose in God's plan, that since we were of the same clay as material reality, then it was to be taken *ipso facto* that our biological evolution and spiritual awakening both depended on nature and its wondrous beauty for their 'nourishment' in the face of inevitable struggle for completion. ('My child, see this world as a unique training ground in which the spiritual increases all the time, preparing you for that which you and I both long.' Fr John Woolley, *I Am with You*, p.240) Christ's Incarnate life followed the same pattern: born into the world of matter, and through it, grew to physical and spiritual maturity by way of love, suffering and death. ('I am saddened that the world still does not recognise the full significance of My involving Myself, to the limit, in human experience. ... Certainty was wonderfully awakened in those who saw the Divine in an earthly setting, but that is not all... Certainty, rather than mystery, is possible for all who live outside the time of that revelation. This happens when that event is deliberately, and with a sense of wonder, locked away in one's heart.' Fr John Woolley, *I Am with You*, p.134). St Paul and Teilhard de Chardin believed wholeheartedly that Christ, taking on our human nature, ushered in the final and decisive phase of the pleroma. One thought that this was immanent ('...when the last trumpet sounds. It will sound, and the dead will be raised, imperishable and we shall be changed as well.' 1 Cor. 15:51), the other, aeons into the future, when Christ's Second Coming on the clouds of Heaven would be manifesting the metamorphosis which He had been bringing about throughout time in the heart of humankind (Teilhard de Chardin, *Le Milieu Divin*, p.128). Both thought that the spiritual power of Christ's Incarnation was an indispensable mystery to be believed because it is the ultimate source through which we create with Him the new heavens and the new earth.

> For as the new heavens and the new earth I shall make will endure before Me – it is Yahweh who speaks – so will your race and name endure. (Isa. 66:22)

> What we are waiting for is the new heavens and new earth. (2 Pet. 3:13)

> Then I saw a new heaven and a new earth. (Rev. 21:1)

> …this phrase is merely a symbol of the new messianic age. St. Paul, following the lead of Jesus (cf. Matt. 19:28), is more realistic: the whole of creation will one day be freed from the dominance of corruption, renewed and transformed by the glory of God. (Rom. 8:19; JB, Ch. 21, p.449, n. 'b')

This is based on Christian doctrine, which has a double foundation: belief that humanity is pursued by the Divine longing Love and through this Love is brought supernaturally, and through our shared physical strivings, to its final end in Christ. We become God by participation ('did I not say you are gods…'), bound as we are irrevocably to the Unity of all things in Christ.

> …so that the saints together make a unity in the work of service, building up the Body of Christ. In this way we are all to come to unity in our faith and in our knowledge of the Son of God, until we become the perfect Man, fully mature with the fullness of Christ Himself. (Eph. 4:12–13)

> The Word of God, through whom all things were made, was made flesh so that as a perfect man He could save all men and sum up all things in Himself. The Lord is

the goal of human history, the focal point of the desires of history and civilization, the centre of mankind, the joy of all hearts, and the fulfilment of all aspirations. It is He whom the Father raised from the dead, exalted and placed at His right hand, constituting Him judge of the living and the dead. Animated and drawn together in His Spirit we press onwards on our journey towards the consummation of history which fully corresponds to the plan of His love: 'to unite all things in Him, things in heaven and things on earth'. (Eph. 1:10), (GS, n. 38)

The Spiritual Power of Suffering

Without doubt the most difficult area of life to comprehend and yet the most creative in our work of Unity is human suffering. Teilhard taught that in the process of Transforming Union, depending on how each person responds to suffering, it is to be thought of as creative energy. If suffering could be accepted as a positive force for the completion of the Kingdom, this conscious act of acceptance would liberate humanity. This does not mean that relief of suffering and injustice is neglected, no, solutions must be pursued, but the individual, nevertheless, by his or her inner acceptance of the suffering takes humanity forward in its effort towards greater being. Suffering has to be relieved, yes, but it has its own mysterious creative power for bringing about genuine transformation. And death through the Spirit is the ultimate leap forward if accepted as such ('That is why there is no weakening on our part, and instead, though this outer man of ours may be falling into decay, the inner man is renewed day by day. Yes, the troubles which are soon over, though they weigh little, train us for the carrying of a weight of eternal glory which is out of all proportion to them.' 2 Cor. 4:16–18) (Teilhard de Chardin, *Hymn of the Universe*, p.93ff.).

The Spiritual Power of Death

The Christian vision of death is not the end of life but its true beginning ('Life is changed not ended.' Preface from the 'Mass for the Dead'). If our final existence is to be God by participation then our biological reality has to disintegrate in order to be raised up and transfigured as Christ was at His Resurrection (John 20:15; Luke 15:16). However, it is a law of Creation that nothing imperfect can exist in the heavenly dimension. Unlike Christ we need to be purified throughout our earthly life and beyond in death to make room for God. Death is the sublime pathway into Unity in God. We all must take this path, and it is only known to God at what point on this path each of us, having been 'refined' in the Fires of Divine Love, has reached his or her ultimate oneness with God (2 Macc. 12:44–5; 1 Pet. 1:7–9; CCC nn. 1030, 1371).

The Light of the World

Like many mystics down the Christian centuries, Teilhard stresses that experience of the Presence of the Spirit of God in matter is natural to every person given that we are open to its reality. To these mystics there is no dichotomy between the outward structure of material existence and its inner reality. The mystic sees within material existence the depths of all the elements of the world as being the elements of Christ's Universal Body, radiating his Divine life. We bathe in the Divine Light coming to us through the mystics. And yet this is a gift we each can give to the world, but it depends on how determined we are to strive for the natural fulfilment of our own soul and that of the whole of creation for this gift to be seen by others ('I am the light of the world; anyone who follows me will not be walking in the dark; he will have the Light of Life.' John 8:12) (Teilhard de Chardin, *Hymn of the Universe*, pp.88, 89).

BLESSED ARE THOSE

...blessed are those whose hearts were open to be cleansed and prepared to receive the Holy Spirit for a transformation. (Vassula Ryden, *True Life in God*, vol. 12, p.119)

When humanity regains its sense of mystery, its sense of what lies beyond this life, it will grasp the reality of its unity, the purpose of its existence, and its duty to work hand in hand with God to fulfil its destiny as a race, not just as individuals within the race, but the human race as a Body, the Mystical Body of Christ. It will recognise that God has made up His 'Mind' that our race will be Divinised through the painstaking evolutionary working of His Spirit, transforming our humanity, matter and spirit, until the work of total union in Christ is completed. No one knows that time, only God (Matt. 24:36).

We will know the presence of God as the most immediate reality of our lives. Religion will permeate everything we do. There will be no boundaries between where religion begins and ends. We will know that God is lovingly concerned with everything we do. We will be totally at home with God, because we will be part of the worship of the whole world. There will be a sense of completeness which recognises men and women in the context of the whole universe and ends with the integration of the person, body and soul, heart and mind. We will understand the reality of the unity of the whole of creation, God and the universe, saints and angels, men and women. This is a vision, not of a lost world, but a vision of a world which still lies ahead, a gift waiting for us.

ADDITIONAL REFLECTIONS
The Mystical Christ

Jesus took on human nature two thousand years ago at that time in history when the world was moving out from Rome. The Christian Church took Christ in His human and Divine natures to the world. His human nature at the time of His death was mature in the fullest sense of the word. His Divinity is always complete: 'I Am Who I Am' (Exod. 3:4; John 10:36). And yet, St Paul says 'Christ was not fully formed'. St Paul means by that, the Mystical Body of Christ which is being formed throughout the duration of creation (Col. 1:24ff.). He therefore charged himself and the whole Christian Church to 'make up in our bodies what is lacking, or incomplete, in the Mystical Body of Christ' through all the drawbacks, disappointments, tragedies *and blessings* which life presents us with.

Teilhard de Chardin, like St Paul, recognised that Christ's resurrected Body physical and Divine was a Body in the process of becoming. As has been said, the whole cosmos which He created and entered into is the Mystical Body of Christ in formation. The Church in its theology has never really tackled what this means, although individuals have attempted to examine the implications of this. What was still lacking was that part of the creation which was still yet to be divinised through Him, with Him and in Him (doxology in the Mass). All created activity from the beginning has gone through the process of becoming or forming the Mystical Body of Christ by the inexorable rise of the Spirit, or through the power of the Spirit. The Mystical Body of Christ at the consummation or the end of the formation of creation is the whole of creation material and spiritual along with Christ. As St Paul says, the totality of creation is in one great act of giving birth. Therefore the whole process of creation is a holy process from beginning to end. There is no direct opposition between matter and spirit. It is all one great plan from the beginning as God intended it. Christ, whilst remaining distinct from His creation, nevertheless, wished to be part of its unfolding in every aspect, but sin (Heb. 4:16). Human beings appeared very late in the evolution of the universe, but nevertheless at the appointed time Christ took on our nature to be 'the spur' for the continuing evolution of His creation (Gal. 4:4). Christ intended that He was, is, and will be part and parcel of the evolution of His universe. When human persons have done all that is required of them (time is not to be reckoned) then the cosmos will be perfected, Christ in His Mystical Body will be complete, and we will be recognised by the Father as heirs to His Kingdom, we will be gods by participation. We will have completed His Adventure of Love with Him.

The holiness of the evolutionary process will only be recognised when we have learned to love the way God loves, because it is His Infinite and Unconditional Love alone which divinises and transforms the whole of His creation into His Divine Image.

'God's Works of Today':

I will pour out my Spirit on all mankind. Your sons and your daughters shall prophesy, your old men shall dream dreams, and your young men see visions.

(Joel Ch 3:1–2)

And suddenly a sound came from heaven like the rush of a mighty wind and it filled the house where they were sitting. They were all filled with the Holy Spirit, and began to speak foreign languages as the Spirit gave them the gift of speech.

(Acts 2:1-4)

GOD'S WORKS OF TODAY

The biggest danger threatening humankind today is not natural disasters or even war, but spiritual malaise. It is the most deadly because it strikes at the root of our humanity. It creates in us an anti-life mentality. Our desire to live or die becomes relative to each person (Isa. 22:13). God becomes irrelevant and belief in His interventions in history and in our contemporary world is seen as infantile and only for people who cannot stand on their own two feet (Wisd. 2:21, 5:4–5; Matt. 5:13) (Robert Speaight, *Teilhard de Chardin: A Biography*, p.153).

Just as individual heavenly revelations through time are one single revelation over the whole of time, so these revelations have to be seen as the natural experiences of our lives, not something apart from our day-to-day temporal experiences, but a natural and intended way of living, designed so by God because of the deep tenderness He has for each one of us, for the fulfilment of the whole person, body and soul, and for the final unity of the whole Body of Christ, the Church. Our Father in Heaven tells us He desires that we 'remember often' that He is right there, where we are, and that we could not live if we were not with Him, and in spite of our unbelief, He always remains close to us (Associazione 'Dio e Padre Casa Pater', *The Father Speaks to His Children*, p.21).

The numberless apparitions, visions, locutions, mystical insights, inspirations, have each in their own way brought the spiritual, or eternal, dimension into our temporal existence. It is quite clear that heaven and earth are the two realities that go to make up our human existence.

My apparitions are to encourage souls of God's Works: they are a call to return to Us, a warning… Pray that the Holy Church returns as in the beginning, when every Work of God was welcomed without disbelief and contempt, without doubt. Pray that the Holy Church's faith will be renewed again, like in the past, and believe in miracles, apparitions and visions, for this is one way of God speaking to you. (Joel 3:1–3; Acts 5:12–16) (Vassula Ryden, *True Life in God*, nb 1–31, p.299)

…as the Father explained it to you, your heart has been created out of Our Sublime Love to return this Love to Us; your heart from the beginning is filled up only with Our Presence, it is created in such an ineffable way that it should be able to maintain all the Sublime Love, and Sweetness of Our Presence, but if thorns and brambles pierce it, like a perforated cistern it will lose its contents; the thorns are the worries of the world and the lure of riches that can perforate the heart and dry it up from the Life giving Spring… (Vassula Ryden, *True Life in God*, One Volume p.1101)

It is thought that those who have personal experiences of heaven breaking into their day-to-day lives are experiencing something beyond what is normal, or natural, when in fact they are experiencing a most natural communication with the dimension of eternity to which every human person belongs, and in which every human person participates through the gifts of the Spirit which have been given to us for the completion of God's plan of Love for His Creation (1 Cor. 12:11–28).

…I created man for Myself and it is right that I should be ALL for him. Man will not enjoy true happiness except with his Father and Creator, because his heart is made for Me alone… For My part, My love for my creatures is so great that I have no greater joy than that of being among them. (Associazione 'Dio e Padre Casa Pater', *The Father Speaks to His Children*, p.27)

From our Father's own words we know that we do not have to wait for God to enter our lives; He is already there. All people are called, loved, inhabited by His Presence (M.M. Philipon, *The Spiritual Doctrine of Elizabeth of the Trinity*, p.107). Eternity is part and parcel of our daily existence as human beings. God has shown us this throughout history. He has, of set purpose, revealed Himself directly and dramatically to individuals, particularly children. Sometimes, and very often, His revelation has been through Our Lady, at other times through the saints. These are a reminder of the reality of our existence, a call to remember that our true nature is material and transcendent. God tells us, 'Why are you so surprised by what I am saying? Did I not create you in My image? I did this so that you should find nothing strange when you talk on familiar terms with your Father, your Creator and your God. For you have become the children of My fatherly and divine love through My merciful goodness' (Associazione 'Dio e Padre Casa Pater', *The Father Speaks to His Children*, p.32ff.).

It is evident that the exercise of our God-given gift of free will means we can remain earthbound, refusing to live true to our spiritual human nature. Until we realise, and accept, that our existence is a dual existence of temporal and eternal, we will never live the two in a harmonious way… there will be conflict within the individual, either a conscious rejection of the eternal dimension, or a desire to alternate between both. Neither of these paths recognises the world as ordained for the soul's fulfilment. One eventually leads to total unbelief, the other leaves the individual restless and imperfect. 'What is born of the flesh is flesh, what is born of the Spirit is spirit' (John 3:5–8). The Father says, 'Let Me tell you, you will never feel truly free nor truly happy until you recognize Me as your Father and submit to My yoke, to be true children of God, your Father. Why? Because I created you for a single purpose, to know Me, love Me and serve Me, as a simple and trusting child serves its father!' Consequently, '…our freedom increases, because loving what God loves we can do so much more. We would have the desire in us to do great things, noble things, and holy things for we are created to have the capacity to love.' It follows because we are made in God's image, '…we descend from nobility, sovereignty and Majesty' – 'no one can take this away from us'. What can we say about such a lineage! This should overwhelm us. The thought that God has endowed us with the dignity of His heirs should provoke tremendous gratitude in us. 'The Path that God has laid out for us is within everyone's reach' (Vassula Ryden, *True Life in God*, One Volume p.1046). 'We can choose to be united with God or separate ourselves from Him. The opportunities to be happy with Him in this life are there for us, and also everything we do has an eternal significance since our destiny is in eternity, and that is non-negotiable. 'God offers His Kingdom' – 'we either choose life or death, Heaven or hell' (Vassula Ryden, Rhodes *True Life in God Retreat*, Sept. 2012).

There are many examples shown to us over the Christian ages of single-minded individuals who have consciously lived out their earthly lives within the two dimensions of heaven and earth. One such example is John the Baptist, at the beginning of the Christian era. Our Lord said of him, 'Of all men born, none is greater than John' (Matt. 11:11). John the Baptist was aware of the heavenly dimension even in his mother's womb (Luke 1:44). He was therefore no stranger to the transcendent side of his nature. The reality of God within us was what he proclaimed and lived (Luke 3:4–6; John 3:29). He was not searching for God 'out there somewhere', he lived in the Presence of God.

Nearer to our own time is Blessed Elizabeth of the Trinity. She too lived, daily, her life in the Presence of the Whole of Reality, the Blessed Trinity. There was no division or separation between her work in the environment of earth and the environment of heaven – the material and the spiritual are both intertwined (Luke 10:41, 42). Elizabeth says, 'I confide to you the secret which has made my life an anticipated heaven: The belief that a Being whose name is Love is dwelling within us at every moment of the day and night, and that He asks us to live in His company' (M.M. Philipon, *The Spiritual Doctrine of Elizabeth of the Trinity*, p.56). And He tells us, 'I live with them more intimately than a mother with her children' (Associazione 'Dio e Padre Casa Pater', *The Father Speaks to His Children*, p.20).

Living in the realms of heaven and earth simultaneously is the way for our human nature, *the* way God planned this particular manifestation of His Creation. But since God willed that His material creation be perfected there has to be a conscious effort on the part of humankind to allow the heavenly dimension to gradually purify and spiritualise the material dimension. This is done by living in the way that best suits our human nature. God has given us all the laws and spiritual guidance we need for us to allow our free will to be transformed by the Holy Spirit into images of the Blessed Trinity. 'For where your treasure is, there will your heart be also' (Matt. 6:21). And the treasure of our hearts is proven by our actions because as we work and live our day-to-day lives as best we can in love, they will be sanctified.

Responsibility of the Church and every individual for the bringing of the Kingdom of God

Our Lady down the ages has been and still is the constant prime example and reminder to the Christian people of just what each person's part is in this world in order to transform it into the new heavens and the new earth (2 Pet. 3:13–15). She above all lived consciously in both these realms. Every apparition is always a contemporary word meeting the needs of the time, and it is always Christ's message for the whole Church, it is no different than that taught through the Gospel. Every authentic apparition is given to us as a definite opportunity to grow in love of God and neighbour, and should not be taken lightly or simply ignored, *which so often happens*. Our Lady's apparitions have done more to blend heaven with earth, and to preserve the faith than any other evangelising effort of the Church.

In her apparitions Our Lady speaks with authority. She urges us, through the power of the Holy Spirit, to take hold of our responsibility for the Church and the world in unveiling the Kingdom on earth with the sole purpose of bringing one another to heaven. After all, this is the main work of our existence. She demands that we act. Christian people should be prepared, like others, to take courage and meet the dangers that the world throws at us, as others do who are not Christian. We more than they should know what our part in the world is. The Church, and in particular the Pope, ought to teach the peoples to be gentle and more open-minded in their judgements of people and situations. To bring people to faith the Church has to present Christ anew by making fundamental changes to *practice*, but *not* in *belief.* Practice must be such that it does not become a yoke around the neck but an encouragement to live as God wants, unburdened and purposeful.

Knowing full well that the Second Vatican Council would take place, she begged the Church authorities to seize the opportunity for change in the spirit of the times ('don't put new wine into old skins, no, new wine, new skins', Mark 2:22). The doctrine, *which is correct*, must now address the modern world in such a way that it speaks to the heart of all the people, developed and less developed nations alike. The struggle must be to bring the peoples into one mind and one spirit.

Our Lady reminds us that in the hidden working of true Love, even the 'important' ones in society will succumb. The struggle is not confined to politics and material concerns, it must always involve the spirit of each person.

The prophet and mystic, Teilhard de Chardin, a man chosen for our times, reflects these very teachings of Our Lady in his inspired writings as he presents 'Christ anew' to the Church, to every Christian and to the world.

To the Church
His thoughts on the modernisation of the Church reveal the same kind of fundamental rejuvenation, which Our Lady asks for, in ecclesiastical structures which have stagnated after two thousand years. He hoped that a rejection of outdated structures be replaced by a forward-looking framework which would produce a spiritual renewal in thinking and worship (Matt. 5:7–8). God would no longer be seen as the 'manager', but would become the heart which beats for the world and its progress, exactly what the peoples are searching for.

He believed firmly that the Church was God's tool in

bringing about the necessary developments of our race and the natural world. But he was disenchanted with the slow pace of reform, which he felt had to come. As Church, we are the children of light but have failed in our responsibility because we have imprisoned the spirit (Robert Speaight, *Teilhard de Chardin: A Biography*, pp.223, 256) (Matt. 5:14–16).

The Church's dogma attributes to Jesus the summit of an evolving universe (CCC nn. 280, 302). He alone is the One who gives meaning to the world by making evolution possible: 'through Him, with Him and in Him' (doxology of the Mass).

Discussing Christianity from the ultimate perspective of God the 'first' scientist, Teilhard develops that truth which spells out that the fundamental relationship of our being with Jesus is one of Transformation into Him. This process which has been, through time, the moving force of human progress has not been recognised as such, nor has it been acknowledged due to our lack of belief in God and our view that the universe has no purposeful and ultimate direction.

The whole process of transformation is a personalising one. The total Mystical Body of Christ will be when we have, as a race and as individuals, together with the whole of cosmic matter, reached the end of universal evolution – a consummated universe where we each will be fully ourselves whilst being one and undivided with the Blessed Trinity and the whole creation (Rom. 8:20–23).

He takes this idea a stage further and explains that it is pre-eminently the priesthood through which this transformation and progress is able to take place, because it is during the sacrifice of the Mass, and essentially the Consecration of the Bread and Wine which ultimately 'transubstantiates' the whole of creation, thereby revealing why God becoming man was necessary if humankind were to become, through the transforming Spirit, god by participation. It works something like this: everything which is undertaken intentionally or unintentionally and which in some way benefits humanity gradually sanctifies the universe ('whatever you do to the least of these, you do it to Me', Matt. 25:40) raising it to union with God. Everything worthwhile which is undertaken bears the value of holiness and communion. The bread and wine at the altar are not only symbols which represent the whole of matter and our efforts, but are the substance through which the cosmos and human actions are consecrated because they have become the Body and Blood of Christ.

St Paul tells us precisely this, the Incarnate Christ is everything and in everything (Col. 3:11; CCC nn. 280, 359; GS 22:1). And the message the risen Christ Himself gives that He is living in us and in the world, and we in Him, bound for all eternity in Love has no competitor (John 14:2–3). No other person has drawn such a vast number of people into a personal relationship as Christ has, and no one can draw us into a personal relationship with the angels and saints. That can only be done by God (John 15:5).

Teilhard views the Cross, and our acceptance of it, as an indispensable means for humanity's development. With optimistic eyes he adds a profound prophetic nuance to the Church's theological understanding of the Cross. Though our falling and rising are made secure by Our Lord's suffering and death, a sign of God's infinite goodness and love, we must, nevertheless, acknowledge that Love, and bravely play our part in the struggle. Since God understood what He created (to say other would be a contradiction in terms), He clearly understood our weaknesses and gave us the remedy of carrying our own cross for personal and universal progress.

Let us listen first of all to our Heavenly Father expressing this in more traditional language: 'The CROSS is My way of coming down among My children, since it is through it that I caused My Son to redeem you. And for you, the Cross is the way to ascend to My Son, and from My Son to Me. Without it you could never come to Me, because man, by sinning, brought on himself the punishment of separation from God' (Associazione 'Dio e Padre Casa Pater', *The Father Speaks to His Children*, p.16).

Teilhard takes what Our Heavenly Father says and enlarges on it thus: the Cross is without equal the most sacred symbol of our redemption but it is also the symbol of victory and progress as humanity unites its labours and sufferings with those of Jesus for the salvation of the world. God did not wipe out all that had gone before Christ's Incarnation, Death and Resurrection. On the contrary, He took a huge risk in planning from the outset a great adventure for His creation, an almighty struggle through the ages to perfect it and save it. And never did He have any other intention than being fully involved from its very beginning to its evolutionary victorious end (Robert Speaight, *Teilhard de Chardin: A Biography*, p.192).

To every Christian

Through Teilhard's unshakeable belief in the future and the consummation of the whole cosmos in Christ, he strives to awaken in the Christian community a vision of Christianity as it really is, an encounter with beauty, the possibility of a more authentic, more exciting life. Without this vision we will not as individuals, and consequently as a world community, take our race forward to its eventual fulfilment as the Mystical Body of Christ. Even today, Christians are reluctant to think in terms of our journey being an evolutionary journey. God's plan of creation is not a static one, but unfolding through time, a momentous universal transformation which takes the whole of time to come about, and in which every human generation has played its part and will play its part. God has offered each of us the opportunity, from the most primitive civilisations to the most developed civilisations of the future, to work to bring about the new heavens and the new earth, hand in hand with Him, co-redeemers with Him. In our relationship of oneness with God we hold back progress when our relationship is one of sterile fear of offending Him. Christianity has largely emerged from its medieval view of the origins of the universe, but the Gospel for too long has been presented as laws to keep at the expense of the beauty and purpose of Creation and its part, as St Paul reminds us, in the whole transformation journey in Christ (Luke 11:52; Col. 1:15–20; GS 45, 93). Our relationship should be a joyous and vigorous collective effort to open up the way forward for the next generation, so that they and successive generations can build the future on life that is real and love that is real and not as we experience it in our own time. ('I have come that you may have life and have it to the full.' John 10:10). We should truly be ministers of the future of the world, of the future of every person.

If there is no development in the individual Christian's conviction about each person's responsibility for bringing the Kingdom, then transformation has and will be arduous with much self-inflicted pain. Material progress for its own sake results in the inevitable mechanisation of peoples. Similarly if Christians remain tepid in their belief in the future they will neglect to nurture the transcendent side of their nature and will remain inert and earthbound.

Love is the energy which brings about transformation, and for Teilhard, the image of the Sacred Heart of Jesus is both the symbol and Source of that energy. We can see the depths of love to which creation is called in the lives of those who apply heart and soul to giving themselves to the fight in building the new heavens and the new earth. To illustrate how this love radiates and affects the individual and the world there is no finer example than the words of St Therese of Lisieux:

> Considering the mystical body of the Church, I had not recognized myself in any of the members described by St Paul, or rather I desired to see myself in them *all*. *Love* gave me the key to my *vocation*. I understood that if the Church had a body composed of different members, the most necessary and most noble of all could not be lacking to it, and so I understood that the Church had a *Heart and that this Heart was BURNING WITH LOVE*. *I understood it was Love alone* that made the Church's members act, that if *Love* ever became extinct, apostles would not preach the Gospel and martyrs would not shed their blood. I understood that LOVE COMPRISED ALL VOCATIONS, THAT LOVE WAS EVERYTHING, THAT IT EMBRACED ALL TIMES AND PLACES… IN A WORD, THAT IT WAS ETERNAL! Then, in the excess of my delirious joy, I cried out: O Jesus, my Love… my *vocation*, at last I have found it… MY VOCATION IS LOVE! (St Therese of Lisieux, *Story of a Soul*, p.194. © ICS Publications)

Teilhard's own words of calm and serenity can be said to sum up the fiery words of St Therese:

> …success may crown our enterprises, joy may dwell in our hearts and all around us, and what sorrow cannot be spared us be transfigured into a finer joy, the joy of

knowing that we have occupied each his own station in the universe and that, in that station, we have done as we ought (1 Tim. 6:11–16). (Robert Speaight, *Teilhard de Chardin: A Biography*, p.187)

To the World

Teilhard, whilst being an optimist, nevertheless warned of the consequences of apathy and disengagement from the real world we live in. He was very aware that humanity's worst danger was not natural or man-made disasters but the lack of appetite for living as a consequence of spiritual malaise (Matt. 5:13). To reject religion is to fatally ignore the fact that, down the ages, humanity has given God His place in material reality through their collective experience. Sometimes more rationally than others, but still, God has 'spoken' and 'written' with crooked lines His Being and His purpose for His creation (Ps. 8:4–6; Wisd. 7:22–30).

We will only recognise God's beauty and the task He has set for His Creation through the Spirit, and in obedience to the inspirations of the Spirit. Only through allowing the Holy Spirit to form the spirit of the individual will lasting progress be made. The energies of love will slowly win out and humanity will experience the Fire of the Spirit which transforms all things in Christ.

A Call to the Church, the individual Christian and the World to live a True Life in God in keeping with our nature as God created us

Our striving to play our part in the bringing of the Kingdom is the privilege which God gives each of us at our creation. Fortunately for us though, when we fail to work in harmony with God's plans, He works independently of us. And where we fail to complete the tasks He gives us, He 'supplies' for us. In the *True Life in God* messages, given to Vassula Ryden, Prophet, Visionary and Mystic, God reassures us (as He does in Scripture and in His communications with us throughout time) that, in spite of our neglect to play our part, He will bring about our renewal in the Spirit.

Our Lady speaks to us about this in the *True Life in God* messages:

> …Ecclesia [the Church] will revive and in the end Our Hearts will prevail. My apparitions are to encourage souls of God's Works; they are a call to return to Us, a warning. This year [1988] I shall appear to many; visions I shall give and visionaries there will be. Pray that the Holy Church returns as in the beginning, when every Work of God was welcomed without disbelief and contempt, without doubt. Pray that the Holy Church's faith will be renewed again, like in the past, and believe in Miracles, apparitions and visions, <u>for this is one way of God speaking to you.</u> Ask for a renewal.

Our Lord complains to Vassula that His Work in the world through His messages to chosen souls is not being accepted in faith, but is continually put aside because of a lack of trust. Some in the Church's hierarchy seem to doubt that God is constantly at work for us, giving us opportunities to reach all peoples through the various means He uses to speak to every person. We are not like peas in a pod, and so He deals with us like the best of fathers who knows and loves each of his children intimately and treats each with meticulous sensitivity for their personal growth. That is why throughout history God has given the human race abundant and different approaches to life in the Spirit – more than enough for every individual to get to know Him intimately, which is His plan and deepest desire since our creation.

Our Lord condemns this lack of faith in His Works of today, and in distress says:

Vassula – I Am. Look at Me, soul. I find no holiness in them. Yes, none. Every time I cry from My Cross, it is that at this same instant I see one of My own giving way to Satan (John 15:24, 25).

And then, in complete harmony with Scripture and in the language of Scripture, after God admonishes, reminding us of our waywardness, He promises us that all will be well:

I give you My Peace and My Love, My child. Ecclesia shall revive in spite of all the tribulations she is undergoing [Matt. 16:18–19]. My Church will be one and holy and My People shall speak one language, all these things shall soon take place [Acts 2:1–13].

Vassula, I shall rise again My Church out of My Everlasting Love and Mercy, I am going to give you all back your vineyards and make out of this valley of death a gateway of Hope and you shall all respond to Me as once before as you did when you were young and pure [Hos. 2:16—6] to pasture and let everyone who has been branded on the forehead with the Sigh of My Love come forward and eat from the Tree of Life. Today I am giving everyone a chance to hear plainly My Voice from My Holy dwelling place, My Voice sounds like an echo from Jerusalem and reaches all the inhabitants of the earth. No one can say later on that I have not been warning you, from nation to nation I let My Spirit blow [John 3:8]. I am sending you all My servants, the prophets, so persistently [Matt. 23:34] to remind you who is your Father and to turn you away from your evil doings and amend your actions. I come to stop you from idolizing theories that are godless. I am sending My messengers to you to remind you of My precepts and to remind you to live holy as I am Holy [Lev. 19:2], so that you will all be worthy to face Me on the Day of My Return [Matt. 24:44]. [Vassula Ryden, *True Life in God*, nb 32–58, p.185]

Those who prefer their own intellectual interpretation of God's Works of Today need to acquire simplicity of spirit and an open heart which adores God before any other activity. Refusing to believe that God is 'alive and active' in His Church, here and now through His prophets of Today, is a rejection of the Holy Spirit rebuilding the Church, and is a sign that in truth those people who resist the transforming Spirit remain only with the earth and have only this life on their horizon.

On the other hand, there are those who do not know God yet, but whose hearts God can read, and who will accept God's Works of Today by responding to the invitation of the Holy Spirit. Who is willing to give them this invitation? Where are the shepherds?

Our Lord addresses His consecrated priests on the subject with these strong words:

I Am. Peace be with you. Honour Me by imitating Me; glorify Me by loving Me. Sanctify your body, since I live in you, by eating Me and by drinking Me. Adore Me, thirst for Me, amend for those who do not love Me and are blinded by their intellect and who cannot tell their right hand from their left (Jonah 4:11). Pray that they may realize that they need perception so as to not deviate, like many of them do, now from My Words. Pray that they may understand that what I want from these wise men is adoration, I want them to come and do Me homage like the first shepherds and like the Magi (Ps. 72:9–11; Matt. 2:11–12).

And you who are consecrated souls to Me, you who represent Me, I tell you this, do you remember how I heard Elijah's complaint to Me about Israel's behaviour? and how he believed that they had killed all My prophets and broken down all My altars? Do you remember what My answer was to that? I said, 'I have kept for Myself seven thousand men who have not bent the knee to Baal (1 Kgs 19:14–18). And today I am telling you beloved brothers: I have kept for Myself a remnant, chosen and transformed by My Grace to remain faithful to Me. This remnant I am raising up to rebuild the altars that once were and reconstruct My Sanctuary, they are the builders of My New Church. So whilste the wicked are continuing their evil deeds – persecuting you, My prophets and My saints of the end of Times, and whilste the proud are struggling for worldwide authority, I, your Redeemer, am raising up and training these builders in My Sacred Heart, to be the pillars of My Church (Rom. 11:3–10).

And how many of the high priests and scribes lent an ear to Me and were positive, only yesterday? Vassula, there is a remnant chosen by grace to believe. Scriptures say: I revealed Myself to those who did not consult Me (Rom. 10:20) yet from the very beginning I have invited everyone to My School:

My Holy Spirit is your Guide,
your Husband and your Master

I tell you truly that soon I will gather all nations in a circle of Love and My Spirit will dwell in you giving sight to the blind, since the Light that will be given you is My Transcendent Light; but how hard it is for those who have accumulated riches in their spirit to penetrate into My Light! How hard it is for the wise to penetrate into the Spirit and perceive Its depths! How hard it is for them to enter into My Kingdom! I tell you solemnly, the rejects of your society and those you call unworthy are making it before these; yes! Those who could not tell good from evil, those who could not tell their left hand from their right! I have been and am still inviting everyone to sit at table with Me, but many have not responded to My invitation, they laughed and scorned at My Gracious Call and caused others who wanted to come, stumble by their teaching. Compare all this with My parable of the wedding feast (Matt. 22:1–14).

I will come back

and they will tremble; they will tremble when they will realize Whom they were rejecting all this time. They renounced My Spirit and allowed themselves to be guided by their own spirit, they renounced My Light for their own, they renounced My Heavenly Knowledge given by Wisdom for a second-rate philosophy and their own rational knowledge;

– they have apostatized –

Since they have rejected My Spirit, My Light and My Knowledge, I shall take away My Kingdom from them and give it to a people who can produce its fruit; I shall then welcome these people as My own and ask them to come with Me and keep house with Me; in fact this hour is here already; I have decided to draw near Me the disreputable, those that hang around on every street corner, the unworthy, the nothing of the nothings, the wretched and those who never knew My Name; I will turn to a wretched lot who never loved Me and make a nation of Love out of them, a holy nation, and they will glorify Me. They will be called priests of the Living God, priests of the Amen, and in this priesthood I shall rebuild My Church, in these hearts I shall unite you all, and My Body will rest. The hour is here, and no one can stop this hour of My Holy Spirit. When you will see the world disintegrating under your feet, when you will look to your left and see tottering kingdoms and cities reduced into a heap of dust and to your right mountains tumbling, know that these signs are the beginning of the outpouring of My Holy Spirit; when you see My pupils whom I Myself have formed, preach fearlessly in My Name, do not disrupt them, resist your temptation and discern the sound of their footsteps, I will keep sending you these saints to gather on their way all the severed members of My Body, and no one, not even the unclean spirits would be able to stop them, these will instead fall down before them because they will know that the Amen is their Master.

The Amen is soon with you My child He who is your Consoler and whose Home is in inaccessible Light will eventually plunge you into His Light and absorb you;

– I am Love –

(Vassula Ryden, True Life in God, nb 32–58, p.391)

Yes, daughter, I asked 'Is it against the Law to cure a man on the Sabbath or not?' – they did not answer. I said, 'Which of you here, if his son falls into a well, or ox, will not pull him out on a Sabbath day without hesitation?' and to this day they could find no answer (Luke 14:1–6). Today I am asking those who refuse this revelation this question: 'is it against My Law in your era to save My creation from falling by My Providential Works of today?' Vassula, I am Jesus and Jesus means Saviour. (Vassula Ryden, *True Life in God*, nb 1–31, p.256)

Our Lady frequently reminds us that the Sacred Heart of Jesus and Her Immaculate Heart are centres of Love and Power from which we detach ourselves at our peril. Estranged from our heavenly home we become detached from our true nature, which results in disintegration in relationships, chaos in our affairs and deep unhappiness, depression and despair. We will only blossom if we live our lives from within the Heart of our Heavenly Father, Who is Love beyond compare:

Write My daughter: blessed of My Soul, beloved of My Heart, today I ask each one of you to apply your heart to walk with God. God is your Strength, your Life and your Happiness, no man can live without God. Jesus is the True Vine and you the branches. A branch cut off from the Vine dries and withers immediately, it is then of no use but to be thrown on the fire (John 15:1–6). Walk with the Light and do not be afraid in abandoning yourselves entirely to Him, give yourselves to God and your hearts shall be filled with Joy (John 8:12). Understand, beloved children, that God in these days is coming to save you and untangle you from Satan's nets and bring you back to His Sacred Heart. Our Two Hearts are united in spite of the arguments and the denials of the world for this Truth, for they have not all accepted this Truth but use this Truth instead to combat one another. Our Two Hearts are united and thirst together for your salvation, children. Come and hear Us this time: make Peace with God, be reconciled, Lift your face to God and ask Him to fill your heart with His Light. Learn to love God as your Father, He who loves you more than anyone can imagine and without ceasing sends you from His Heart His flowing Peace, like a River to assuage the interior desert of your soul. Do not live out of words only, act and live every word given to you in the Gospels. Do not be dead at the letter of the Law, live it. Do not be afraid if anybody mocks you or refuses to believe in the Wonders God is giving you today, for I tell you: if anyone reduces you to silence, the stones will cry out all the harder. Only God can give you Peace and Happiness. I am praying for you without ceasing so that from hard stones this generation's heart can turn to God and be like a watered garden; from an uninhabited desert, a Holy City full of God's Light, a Light coming from God, and not by sun or moon. After the storm will be over and gone, flowers will spring up, changing the surface of this earth. I, your Holy Mother, bless each one of you. (Vassula Ryden, *True Life in God*, nb 32–58, p.324)

God's Loving Mercy holds us in existence. Without His moment-by-moment understanding and forgiveness we could not exist. People who live without God imagine they remain on this earth by their own efforts, when experience of life shows us that life can be taken away at any moment. If we have no control over the time of our death, we should ask ourselves, 'who is really in charge of our lives' and in complete confidence leave our future under God's loving control? This does not leave our own perception unimpaired but helps us make wise choices. It does not take us out of the present but enriches the present (Fr John Woolley, *I Am With You*, p.191).

> Peace be with you. I have come all the way to you to tell you
>
> I am here.
>
> Beloved, My Sacred Heart is on Fire, this is why I descend from My Throne to come all the way to you and offer you My Peace and My Love. Mercy is at your doors. If there were two knees to receive you with great love at your birth and two arms to hug you with affection, I tell you, I have done more than that, I have laid down My Life for you. I am the Source of Love. Come, renounce all that stains your soul and follow Me. Do not say, 'my way of life is faultless'. You are without beauty and without majesty so long as your soul is stained and imperfect. Come, I can perfect your soul since I am offering you free and at no cost My Blood and My Flesh. Surrender yourself to Me, I am the Life. (Vassula Ryden, *True Life in God*, nb 32–58, p.325)

Mother of us all

Our Lady is Mother of us all regardless of our faith or none. In her apparitions, she comes to awaken us to the heedlessness of our spiritual poverty. In Her Motherly protection she gives us warnings, but at the same time encouragement. Nevertheless, her warnings should be taken seriously as they are given to us in our day to learn how to reject evil and to do good.

The peoples, particularly in the West, have grown away from the acceptance of evil forces in the world which act upon us in a negative way, destroying our will to be good. And yet, we have known of the existence of evil since the very beginning and that God planned to deal with it. The person chosen by God to crush the cause of evil is Mary, Mother of all nations, through Her authority as Co-redemptress with Christ, our Redeemer. She it is who will fulfil the first prophecy of Salvation in Scripture by crushing Satan at the appointed time (Gen. 3:14, 15). Our Lady throughout the life of the Church has warned us of our indifference to the reality of evil and its consequences which we see all around us every day. The fact that Satan has not been able to rid creation of faith in God means that Our Lady has, in the age of the Church, been given the authority by Her Son to 'crush Satan's head with her heel', keeping him in check. The end of his time of darkness and sin is set by God and *will* come about. Our Lady emphasises that the power of Satan is conditional on our response to grace. He has no power over us at all if we depend on God.

Even Our Lady's visionaries have found difficulty in responding immediately to God's wishes because of the pressure of the world on them to conform to worldly reasoning. Passing on Our Lady's messages to the world involves putting honour to God before honour to men. This is a struggle for visionaries and also those who wish to live the life of the Spirit because they experience opposition from family and friends, their superiors in the Church and the scepticism of people in general.

In the last decades of the twentieth century there came a multitude of eastern and new age religions, leading people into a false understanding of God. Our relationship with God no longer was with the Three Persons of the Trinity, Father, Son and Holy Spirit, the ground and future of our being. Instead, it became a relationship with the world, a pantheistic, hedonistic, individualist, unreal and impersonal belief without purpose or meaning for our existence.

Our Lady comes to us to help us open our eyes to our situation. We have severed links with reality. Humankind's God-given ingenuity meant for the progress of the peoples has so often been used for self-gain. In the name of so-called progress our worldly wisdom has brought us to the point where we are unable to find a remedy for the many harmful inventions which deal a blow to our environment and suppress our spirit. Our Lady tells us the only remedy is to reconnect with God through prayer – 'let Him become your Faithful Friend'!

Holy Spirit, Source of Transformation for the World

'Transformation really means a change in the way you see the world – a shift in how you see yourself. It is not simply a change in your point of view, but rather a whole different perception of what is possible' (Francis Vaughan). In the context of the whole dimension of our lives it requires a vision of what it will mean to realise the 'immense wishes, the range of the enterprise, its greatness, its breadth and its depth' at the heart of God's plan for His creation (Eph. 3:18–19). It will mean the development of personal responsibility for the Unity of all peoples in Christ through the transforming work of the Holy Spirit. The transforming action of the Holy Spirit necessarily involves a spiritual battle. A struggle to correct within ourselves all those self-centred, ingrained habits and those potentially deadly skirmishes with the world of evil spirits is inevitably at the heart of our transformation if the triumph of the new heavens and the new earth is to come. And this battle is necessary for the fulfilment of God's dream for His

Creation. In our era, it is at its most ferocious, and unwittingly or wittingly we are all participants.

> Everyone must understand that there are important elements at stake in this Battle for every man and woman. Everyone is engaged into this spiritual Battle, and it is not a Battle of flesh and blood, but of spirit. Our Battle is with spiritual powers, spiritual beings, that influence us and tempt us to do evil. They infest our minds to do the wrong thing.
>
> Evil does everything it can to destroy our soul and to damage God's creation; wars, crime, hatred, nation against nation greedy for power.

(Extracts from Vassula Ryden's talk on 'The Spiritual Battle', Rhodes True Life in God Retreat, Sept. 2012)

To eradicate evil there must be a conscious effort on our behalf to live daily in our natural environment of heaven and earth, in other words, in the presence of God, in the Holy Spirit, who is our Maker and the most intimate and loveable of all fathers who constantly thinks of us and has our concerns, our sorrows and dejections within His Heart. He so much desires to share His intimacy with us.

'The meaning of our lives is to love God and to be like God to be with Him forever. God is beautiful beyond all human imagination' (Vassula Ryden, Rhodes True Life in God Retreat, Sept. 2012). And yet our Heavenly Father is so often portrayed as a frightening old man waiting to strike us with His thunderbolts. With majestic humility He draws our attention to this image of Himself in His Message to Sister Eugenia, 'Do not think of Me as that frightening old man whom men depict in their pictures and books! No, no, I am neither younger nor older than My Son and My Holy Spirit. Because of this I would like everybody, from the youngest to the oldest, to call Me by the familiar name of Father and Friend. For I am always with you, I am making Myself similar to you so as to make you similar to Me. How great would be My joy to see parents teaching their children to address Me often by the name of Father, as indeed I am! How I would like to see infused into these young souls a trust and a filial love for Me! I have done everything for you; will you not do this for me?' (Associazione 'Dio e Padre Casa Pater', *The Father Speaks to His Children*, p.22).

The Sacraments, our means of Transformation
Crucial for our transformation to enable us to take personal responsibility for the Unity of all peoples in Christ is made clear by Our Lady. We are to live our faith fully by receiving the Sacraments, and particularly the Eucharist and Reconciliation. The Mass par excellence is the gift Our Lord promised us when He said He would not leave us orphans, but would remain with us forever (John 14:15–18). He gave it so that we could receive Him every day. It is a strange thing that we do not wish to receive God every day! The effects of receiving the Sacraments should be that we become evangelisers, bringing children, men and women to God, and back to the Sacrifice of the Mass. Firstly by the way we live our lives, but importantly by talking about what is most natural in our lives, God, since He created our human nature and became one of us so that we would share His Divine Nature and become god by participation. It might not be realised, but atheists and humanists talk far more about God, albeit negatively, than Christian people do. We must go to the Holy Spirit for guidance, or else transformation will not

take place, and it will not be possible for us to reach out to the lost sheep and bring them back to God. Our Lady reminds the whole Church of their responsibility of bringing the Kingdom of God, and urges us to act accordingly.

Unity of All Nations in the Church with One Heart and One Mind

Our transformation through the Holy Spirit from a divided Church giving confused witness, to a Church which worships the Holy Trinity with One Heart and One Mind, a community of all nations gathered around the One Altar, this is the cry of Christ at the Last Supper (John 17:10).

In spite of our infidelities and neglect, Our Father in heaven pursues us with loving kindness. And because Our Lady and Our Lord have experienced a human existence, great sorrows and the Cross, they know how to deal with our shortcomings. As has already been said, the human race has been given the gift of ingenuity, but so many of our scientific inventions and discoveries have been used to divert and even destroy human progress, deepening our disunity in terms of wellbeing and creating spiritual lethargy. Humankind has obscured God's plan from the beginning, and over time, delaying our becoming the One Body of Jesus Christ. In that Body we would function as One Community for the glory of God and our earthly happiness as we move towards our eternal destiny in the realm of the Blessed Trinity. Life's reverses are made more bearable, and we can see a way through when we deliberately share these with Heaven, because Our Lady and Our Lord have travelled this road before us.

After Unity of the churches has come there will be the promised period of peace, but before this we will notice that discord and dissension will gradually disappear. However, this period of harmony among the nations will last only as long as we adhere to the way shown us by God. When we begin to assert our own will over the will of God then things will start to go wrong again, because we will have once again wandered out of God's embrace.

Some Christians and non-Christians do not like the honour which Catholic and Orthodox Christians accord to the Mother of God; but it is precisely because *She is* the Mother of God that She is held in higher esteem than any other mortal. Our Lady's position given Her by God is not to be questioned – that is their relationship whether we like it or not. Love and fidelity characterised Her whole earthly life, and She has never been absent from the era of the Church, She has only been totally present and active for God's Glory and our salvation. This is a vital area for God's Works of Today for Christian Unity in which we must allow the Holy Spirit, Who is the 'Spouse' of Our Lady, to transform our heart and mind if we are to have the right relationship with the Blessed Trinity, because if we cannot acknowledge Mary as Mother of God we cannot relate to the Three Persons by Whom She is loved so much. Whilst this message is serious, it cannot fail to be joyous because through it we learn of the wonderful harmony between Heaven and earth. As Our Lady tells us, we must be willing to reflect on Her words and believe in them in order to see the signs of this harmony brought about by the Holy Spirit (Luke 1:26–38; The Nicene Creed).

The Word of God

Heaven's word too is within us. Just as the words of others become part of us, so does the Word of God become part of our being, Jesus says:

> My Peace I give to you. I am the Lord and willingly I am providing you with food from heaven. Write My dove, write these words from Scriptures:

'If you remain in Me and My Words remain in you, you may ask for whatever you please and you will get it.' (John 15:7)
Listen and write: in mercy I have pitied you and this is why I am here to instruct the uninstructed and to give My Law to the lawless. I shall continue to feed this generation on the heritage of My Father in Heaven – the Bread that cures you comes from above; the Bread of instruction descends from heaven, from My Father's stores. No one should say: 'I have nothing to eat' – here I am offering it to you so that you do not get tempted to eat what is vile and deadly, that which comes from the root of the world. My Spirit is offering you life and peace. I am writing these few words to you through My flower (Vassula Ryden, *True Life in God*, vol. v, pp.34–5).

Words from those who have gone before us

Those heavenly creatures present here with us will have the last word on the presence of God in our lives:

Our Lady
…as the Father explained it to you,
your heart has been created out of Our Sublime Love
to return this Love to Us;
your heart from the beginning is filled up only with Our
Presence,
it is created in such an ineffable way
that it should be able to maintain all the Sublime Love,
and Sweetness of Our Presence,
but if thorns and brambles pierce it, like a perforated
cistern
it will lose its contents;
the thorns are the worries of the world and the lure of riches

that can perforate the heart and dry it up from the Life
    giving Spring…
(Vassula Ryden, *True Life in God*, one vol., p.101)

Blessed Elizabeth of the Trinity

'Let us live with God as with a friend. Let us make our
Faith alive in order to live in communion with Him
through everything. Our Heaven we carry within us, for
He who is the joy of the blessed in the clear light of
vision, gives Himself to us in faith and mystery. But He
is the same! I have found my heaven on earth, for heaven
is God and God is within me. On the day I understood
this, everything became radiant for me. I would like to
whisper this secret to all I love, so that they, too, may
remain always near to God through everything. Then the
prayer of Christ becomes a reality: "Father, may they be
one in us" (John 17:11–26)' (Fr Keon de Meester, *An
Introduction to Elizabeth of the Trinity*, p.8).

'When we look at the divine world which enfolds us,
even here in our exile and in which we can move, how
the things of earth disappear!' (M.M. Philipon, *The
Spiritual Doctrine of Elizabeth of the Trinity*, p.176).

'This intimacy with the One who dwells within me has
been the beautiful sunshine that has irradiated my life'
(Ibid.).

St John of the Cross

'O thou soul, most beautiful of creatures, who so longest
to know the place where thy Beloved is, that thou mayest
seek Him and be united to Him; thou art thyself that very

tabernacle where He dwells, the secret chamber of His retreat where He is hidden. Rejoice therefore and exult because thy Beloved, thy Treasure, thy sole hope is so near as to be within thee; and to speak truly, thou canst not be without Him' (Ibid., p.212).

Final Thought

The reality that heaven blends with earth is an abiding truth, not simply a nice notion of ours. As has been said at the beginning of this little treatise, all Divine interventions are given not only for that time and place, but for all time.

Abbreviations

JB: *The Jerusalem Bible* (1966)

CCC: Catechism of the Catholic Church (1994)

GS: Vatican II Document 'Gaudium et spes' (Pastoral Constitution of the Church in the Modern World) (1965)

Glossary

Biosphere: The area of whatever life on earth is incapable of reflection.

Catechesis: Handing on the Faith to the members of the Church in every age through the words and deeds of God's Revelation.

Cerebralisation: The development (or evolution) of reflective thought in humankind.

Consummation: The final perfecting of the universe in Christ at the end of time.

Eucharist: The source and summit of the Church's life and transformation; the memorial of Christ's Death and Resurrection; the Real Presence of Christ's Body and Blood in the consecrated bread and wine in the Mass.

Hominisation: The process leading to reflective life in mankind.

Incarnation: Jesus enters His creation truly Man whilst remaining truly God.

Logos: A name given to Christ because He is the Wisdom and Thought of our Heavenly Father expressed to us in time.

Mystical Body of Christ: Head and members form one mystical Person, the Total Christ. The unity of the Mystical Body does not do away with diversity within the Mystical Body.

Omega: The point at which the universe will ultimately centre upon itself and the climax of evolution, identified by Teilhard with the risen Christ of the Parousia.

Omnipresence: God is present in all places at the same time.

Ontological: The nature of being or existence. For the purposes of this work, our existence is inseparable from the Being of God.

Parousia: The Second Coming of Christ.

Participated being: Human persons sharing in God's nature.

Paschal Mystery: The Life, Death and Resurrection of Jesus accomplished God's saving plan for His Creation – the Paschal Mystery, or Christ's work of salvation, is manifest in the Mass.

Phylum: One of the 12 major subdivisions of the animal kingdom.

Pleroma: The final fullness of all things in Christ that will be accomplished at the Parousia.

Teleology: Explains the goal of history, the future focal point of the whole human community.

Transforming Union: See 'Unitive transformation'.

Transubstantiation: The changing of the whole substance of the bread and wine into the whole substance of the Body and Blood of Christ through the power of the Holy Spirit in the Mass. In this work 'transubstantiates' refers also to the whole cosmos and human action becoming the Body and Blood of Christ.

Ultra-humanisation: The transcending of our human nature by divinisation which can only come about through the action of God's unitive transforming Love.

Unitive transformation: The transforming Love of God bringing us into union with Him, or, making us 'gods by participation'.

Bibliography

Associazione "Dio e Padre Casa Pater", *The Father Speaks to His Children*, (2010) (email: avemaria@armatabianca.org)

H.U. von Balthasar, *Cosmic Liturgy: The Universe According to Maximus the Confessor*, (Ignatius Press, 2003)

Pope Benedict XVI, *Address to the Pontifical Academy of Sciences* (2006)

G. Chapman, *Catechism of the Catholic Church* (Goeffrey Chapman 1994)

P. Teilhard de Chardin, *The Future of Man* (Collins, 1964); *The Heart of Matter* (Harcourt Brace and Company, 1978); *Hymn of the Universe* (Collins, 1965); *Le Milieu Divin* (Collins, Fontana Books, 1965); *Man's Place in Nature* (Collins, Fontana Books, 1973)

R. Faricy, S.J., *All Things in Christ: Teilhard de Chardin's Spirituality* (Collins, 1981)

A. Flannery (ed.), *Gaudium et spes, Vatican Council II: The Conciliar and Post Conciliar Documents* (Fowler Wright Books Ltd, 1980)

A. Flannery (ed.), *Lumen Gentium, Vatican Council II: The Conciliar and Post Conciliar Documents* (Fowler Wright Books Ltd, 1980)

Gertrude of Helfta, *The Herald of Divine Love* (M. Winkworth (ed.), Paulist Press, 1993)

S.O. Horn, S. Wiedenhofer (Comp.), *Creation and Evolution: A Conference with Pope Benedict in Castel Gandolfo* (Ignatius Press, 2008)

A. Jones (ed.), *The Jerusalem Bible* (Darton, Longman and Todd, 1966)

J.A. Lyons, *The Cosmic Christ in Origen and Teilhard de Chardin* (Oxford University Press, 1982)

Fr Keon de Meester, *An Introduction to Sr Elizabeth of the Trinity* (Darlington Carmel)

M.M. Philipon, *The Spiritual Doctrine of Elizabeth of the Trinity* (Teresian Charism Press, Washington DC, 2002)

H. Rahner, S.J., *Greek Myths and Christian Mystery* (Biblo and Tannen, 1971)

J. Ratzinger, *In the Beginning* (William B. Eerdmans, 1995)

V. Ryden, *True Life in God* (Trinitas, 2003)

R. Speaight, *Teilhard de Chardin: A Biography* (Collins, 1967)

St Therese of Lisieux, *Story of a Soul* (ICS Publications, Washington DC, 1996)

E. de Waal (ed.), *The Celtic Vision: Prayers and Blessings from the Outer Hebrides* (Darton, Longman and Todd, 1988)

Fr J. Woolley, *I Am With You* (Crown (Great Britain), ISBN 978-1903816998, 1985)

About the Author

I was born in the North East of England, the youngest of seven children, 69 years ago. My teenage years were normal, happy and carefree. At the age of twenty-two I set off for what was then Rhodesia and is now Zimbabwe, to work as a lay missionary. I met my husband Bernard there, and together we enjoyed three thoroughly interesting years in Missionary schools. That experience was something I have always cherished as one of the most formative and important in my life. Bernard and I have been married for 45 years and have two wonderful sons, a super daughter in law and three lovely grandchildren. Early on in our marriage we felt the attraction of the 'good life' and for 36 years we have produced a great deal of our own food on our small holding in rural Cumbria. Later in life I studied theology and gained a B.Div and an MA in RE and Catechesis. For a small number of years I taught. Largely my life has been lived within the environment of my Catholic faith, as has Bernard's.

Why did I decide to write a book and why did I choose primarily to focus on two persons of faith, Teilhard de Chardin and Vassula Ryden? The simplest and truest answer is that I was being asked by God to bring an echo of the work which God had given each of them to do, to those who wish to learn something of the way God walks with us through life.

Teilhard de Chardin and Vassula Ryden remain signs of contradiction as is the destiny of prophets down the ages. But as with all true prophets what they have to proclaim is inevitably proven to be what is needed for their time and all time, 'Truth is the Daughter of Time'.

Pope John Paul II, Pope Benedict XVI and the Second Vatican Council have very positively commented on or reflected the insights of Teilhard de Chardin. Vassula Ryden has been received warmly by those in authority in her own Orthodox Church, and by Pope John Paul II and Pope Benedict, and likewise Pope Francis when he was Cardinal Bergoglio.